8 SURVIVAL SKILLS FOR CHANGING TIMES

DATE DUE

DEMCO 38-297

*The 1993 Chapel of the Air 50-Day Spiritual Adventure
"Survival Skills for Changing Times"*

8 Survival Skills for Changing Times, by David Mains. Discover eight practical "life preservers," designed to keep your values and your faith intact in a fast-spinning world. Small group discussion questions and helpful excerpts from other books included with each chapter. Catalog no. 6-3036.

Getting Beyond "How Are You?" by David Mains and Melissa Mains Timberlake. Are you desiring closer connections with others? Do you often feel lonely? Learn the art of moving from small talk to significant and healing conversation. Catalog no. 6-3035.

Coming Back, by Steve and Valerie Bell. Gain inspiration from the stories of spiritual survivors, men and women who found God sufficient in their darkest moments and who offer hope for our own times of heartache and struggle. Catalog no. 6-3037.

Adventural Journals. Dig deeper into the Adventure with day-by-day personal growth exercises. Available in the following editions:

Adult	Catalog no. 6-8820
Youth	Catalog no. 6-8821
Children, grades 3–6	Catalog no. 6-8822
Primary, preschool–grade 2	Catalog no. 6-8823

ALSO AVAILABLE:

Adventure Leader's Manual	Catalog no. 6-8824
Children's Church Curriculum	Catalog no. 6-3101

8 SURVIVAL SKILLS FOR CHANGING TIMES

DAVID MAINS

VICTOR BOOKS

A DIVISION OF SCRIPTURE PRESS PUBLICATIONS INC.
USA CANADA ENGLAND

"The ABC Cafe—Red and Black," Lyrics by: Alain Boubil, Jean-Marc Natel, and Herbert Kretzmer.

"Bring Him Home," Lyrics by Alain Boubel and Herbert Kretzmer.

Both from the musical *Les Miserables* by Alain Boubel and Claude-Michel Schonberg.

Our Town by Thornton Wilder, Harper Collins. Copyright 1938, © 1957 by Thornton Wilder. Reprinted by special permission of the estate of Thornton Wilder.

All Scripture quotations are from the *Holy Bible: New International Version®*. Copyright © 1973, 1978, 1984 by International Bible Society. Used by permission of Zondervan Publishing House. All rights reserved.

Copyediting: Barbara Williams
Cover Design: Scott Rattray
Cover Illustration: Robert Bergin

Library of Congress Cataloging-in-Publication Data

Mains, David R.
    8 survival skills for changing times / by David Mains.
        p.   cm.
    Includes bibliographical references.
    ISBN 1-56476-036-7
    1. Christian life—1960— 2. Conduct of life. I. Title.
  II. Title: Eight survival skills for changing times.
  BV4501.2.M3262   1992
  248'.4—dc20   92-29671
                                    CIP

---

1 2 3 4 5 6 7 8 9 10 Printing/Year 96 95 94 93 92

Contents

Dedicated to
Tom and Sherline Dunkerton
in gratitude for
your longtime friendship.

Thank you
for sharing your love of the theater
and for showing me how it often illustrates
God's truth.

INTRODUCTION

Changing times are often the backdrop for good stories.

For example, Tevye, the poor Jewish dairyman in *Fiddler on the Roof,* is caught between the tradition of his people and the will of his more modern daughters. Times are changing. These five young women no longer want marriages arranged by the matchmaker in their small Russian village.

In one scene, Tevye is told by his daughter Chava that she has fallen in love with a young Russian man who is not Jewish. Tevye anguishes over the thought of her marrying outside the faith. "If I try to bend that far," he says, "I will break!"

Even his town is changing. In Anatevka—"Anatevka, dear little village, little town of mine"—the Russian officials make it known that Jews are no longer welcome there.

Changing times—how do people survive them?

Les Miserables is fast becoming the most popular musical of all time. Based on Victor Hugo's novel, its backdrop is France in the early 1800s, where political leaders have become insensitive to the needs of the masses. Anticipating an insurrection, idealistic French university students sing:

There's a river on the run
Like the flowing of the tide
Paris coming to our side!
The time is near!

But they're wrong. The citizens of the city don't rise up. And most of the students die fighting at the barricades they have erected.

This play, like *Fiddler on the Roof,* is marked by a number of prayers. The hero of *Les Miserables* is involved in a most tender scene just before the battle in the streets. Jean Valjean, by this time well into his middle years, asks God to please spare the young student Marius. That's because Cosette, the girl Valjean has raised, is in love with Marius.

God on high,
Hear my prayer [sings Valjean].
In my need
You have always been there.
He is young. He's afraid.
Let him rest, Heaven blessed.
Bring him home . . . let me die [Valjean prays]
Let him live.

Like Tevye in *Fiddler,* Jean Valjean and young Marius in *Les Miserables* want to be survivors.

One of my favorite characters in Scripture is a handsome young student when we first meet him. Raised to be part of the royal court, he is instead deported to Babylon after his home city of Jerusalem is invaded. But because God has given him the ability to interpret King Nebuchadnezzar's dreams, Daniel receives a high position within the Babylonian government. Several times he faces close calls with death because he refuses to worship foreign gods. Once he sees the entire political backdrop change design. What was Babylonian, in an overnight coup, becomes Persian. As we read the account, we hold our breath until Daniel, an experienced survivor, is again made a high ranking official in this new regime.

It's Daniel who prayed these words (after God revealed to him the substance of King Nebuchadnezzar's dream): "[Our Lord] changes times and seasons; He sets up kings and deposes them. He gives wisdom to the wise and knowledge to the discerning" (Dan. 2:21). That's what we need in our day—wisdom and discernment.

You see, in recent years we have witnessed tumultuous changes throughout the world. Few observers would have predicted the speed by which some of these transformations took place. Atheistic Communism was suddenly overthrown in the Soviet Union and the next thing we knew, leaders of the Commonwealth of Independent States were asking the West for moral and spiritual help.

At the same time in many of the Eastern European countries, worn out old backdrops were done away with and new sets were lowered into place—with scenes the church had a hand in painting. God had deposed rulers and changed times and seasons.

What about North America?

For us in North America, what will the next several years bring about? Will we experience a major economic earthquake, as some are predicting? We can't help but observe that in many ways our society is starting to unravel, just as Eastern regimes have come apart. Our families are in serious trouble. Children say, "We don't want to live by the traditions of our parents." Concerned dads and moms respond, "If we try to bend that far, we'll break!"

Many North Americans are losing faith in the political process. Crime is on the increase. The moral decline in America is alarming. And because no nation can sin with impunity, many Christians wonder if judgment isn't coming soon.

Some of the changes in our society are positive. This is a time when Christians are joining together to pray in unprecedented numbers. Like Jean Valjean, we say, "Lord, in our need You have always been there." Perhaps there's a new river on the run . . . a revival river flowing from the temple as the prophet describes in Ezekiel 47. First it's ankle-deep, then knee-deep, then up to the waist, and pretty soon deep enough to swim in—a fast-flowing river bringing life and beauty to all in its path!

One way or the other, you can count on this: Change is difficult, even when it's change for the good. It tends to throw people off balance.

So how do we live through changing times? And, like Daniel, how do we remain faithful to the Lord in the process?

My personal belief is that God makes it possible for His people to be spiritual survivors, even in days of great change. In fact, during such seasons He has written some of His best tales of the kingdom. Our Lord is marvelous at using the backdrop of changing times to speak his lines through characters such as Mordecai the Jew in the Book of Esther.

In this account, Mordecai is trying to persuade Queen Esther to participate in a dangerous plot to save the Jews from death at the hands of the Persians. He says, in effect, "Esther, sure it's a tough spot to be in, but you can be a national heroine. Another day, another place, and that might not be true. You're just another pretty face. But how fortunate you are to have a lead role in this exciting drama. Why, I believe you've come to the kingdom for such a time as this!"

What Is a Spiritual Survivor?
When I use the term *spiritual survivor,* I'm not picturing someone hanging on by his or her spiritual fingertips and in the end just barely making it. Nor do I envision spiritual survivors as Christians who are concerned only about their own welfare.

To me, a spiritual survivor is someone who finds himself or herself in a changing, challenging, and sometimes confusing world, and prays, "Lord, stand with me now. Give me Your wisdom and discernment. And I'll play the role You assign me for all it's worth!"

Spiritual survivors have an attitude that says, "Not somehow, but triumphantly!" That expression comes to me from my years at Wheaton College in Wheaton, Illinois. Then President V. Raymond Edman used to challenge young students to live with great purpose. "Not just somehow, but triumphantly," he would say time and again. "Brave Wheaton sons and daughters true, don't be afraid . . . not somehow, but triumphantly. For Christ and His kingdom."

In that same spirit I want you as a reader to adopt an attitude for the remainder of the '90s that centers on purposeful Christian living. Determine now to live decidedly Christian.

That's important. You see, I'm almost certain the eight survival skills I've chosen to emphasize in this book will stretch you some. They're not simple devotional thoughts you can mull over briefly and then forget. These survival skills require a response on your part that could be a bit discomforting.

I mention that upfront because I'm still trying to adjust to several of them myself. It's not that I'm fighting the Lord, but Jesus' ways don't always come easily for me. And so I pray, "Don't give up on me, Lord!"

The Apostle Paul writes to the Ephesians, "Be very careful, then, how you live—not as unwise but as wise... because the days are evil. Therefore do not be foolish, but understand what the Lord's will is" (Eph. 5:15-17). Here again we notice that need for wisdom and discernment, for understanding.

This book is about acquiring skills that will enable you to live through times of change with your values and your faith intact.

The specific challenges I'll present were first brainstormed by fellow ministers and laypersons who helped me select the biblical truths that would be most relevant and beneficial. I'm grateful for their help. I trust that my work will do justice to their input, because in those meetings there was a distinct sense that the Lord was with us in the process.

All of us believe we are facing days of great change. These could even be the end times, the day when God takes us all home. In whatever circumstances we find ourselves, we are convinced that the Lord makes it possible for His people to be spiritual survivors.

In *Fiddler,* when Tevye's daughter Hodel gets on the train to travel far, far away to Siberia to join her chosen fiancé, she says, "Papa, God alone knows when we shall see each other again." And Tevye responds, "Then we will leave it in His hands."

I don't have a specific word from the Lord for you regarding the future. I too am content to "leave it in His hands"! But I do feel led to challenge us to be better prepared to live in a world of rapid change, and change that isn't always as far, far away as we would like.

CHAPTER ONE
DOWNSCALING

"You made many, many poor people," Tevye the dairy farmer says to God in *Fiddler on the Roof*. "I realize, of course, that it's no shame to be poor, but it's no great honor either!"

Then he begins to daydream. "If I were a rich man . . . " And the thought is so wonderful to him he can't even express it in normal words. "Daidle deedle daidle digguh digguh deedle daidle dum. All day long I'd biddy biddy bum, if I were a wealthy man."

Lots of people feel the same as Tevye. "Lord, how wonderful it would be to have lots of money, to be able to buy whatever I want—to be rich."

As I think about poor people, another man comes to mind. He was impoverished, at least by this world's standards. This man was a storyteller, among other things, and several of his tales warned against Tevye-type desires.

One of these short stories concerned a farmer who had such a Tevye-wish come true. This man's land produced absolutely terrific crops. His acreage was so fertile that after a while he ran out of places to store all the produce.

Mulling things over, the farmer decided to tear down the storage bins and barns he already had in order to build bigger ones. He sang to himself, "I really am a rich man, daidle deedle daidle digguh digguh deedle daidle dum. I have stored up plenty; now I'll rest. I'm for sure a wealthy man. Now that I'm rich I'll eat, and drink, and be merry."

"Oh, no you won't!" God said to him. "You fool! [Luke 12:20] This very night your life will be demanded from you. Then who will get what you have prepared for yourself?"

The farmer wouldn't get to keep what he had. There was

no way he could take his new barns to the next world.

Then verse 21 is a warning to all Tevye-types who think bigger and better is always the way to go. Here Jesus declares, "This is how it will be with anyone who stores up things for himself but is not rich toward God."

According to our Lord in this passage, we need to watch out for an attitude that says, "For the forseeable future I'm finally covered financially. Now it's time to enjoy life a bit. And let's face it, I deserve it! It's about time my Tevye-dreams came true."

For people in my general age bracket, those of us who feel we are at long last starting to get it all together, Christ's words are a timely warning. At the peak of our earning power, some of us can finally buy the kind of house we've always dreamed of, go on the trips we never could afford to take before, or at least enjoy a *taste* of the good life. We may not wish to live the lavish lifestyles of the rich and famous, but we'd like to take a step up at least in the food we eat, the clothes we wear, and the cars we drive.

"Is that so selfish? And Jesus, we're wondering if the problem isn't more in the wording You used? What if we change bigger and better barns to 'wise planning for the future, so we can experience some of God's blessings before we're too old to enjoy them'?"

Maybe wording will solve the problem, and maybe it won't. I know that in another passage Christ said having a lot of money made it difficult for a person to enter heaven. But how much money is a lot? And exactly where on the chart does that "rich" category begin? Then, of course, Jesus didn't say it was *impossible* for the rich to get to heaven—only difficult. So let's just leave it that if we want to be spiritual survivors, money can be a problem. That's true anytime. But it's especially important when everything starts shifting on us.

Downscaling
This book is about survival skills for changing times. The first survival skill we all would do well to consider seriously is downscaling. Downscaling is the opposite of striving toward bigger and better.

Scaling down means that we purposely choose to live on less rather than more—that we realize we have already eaten better and been clothed and transported better than the vast majority of people on this earth. Downscaling means discovering spiritual growth through living less extravagantly and more simply. It means that we stop accumulating and start letting go of things, while at the same time we become marvelously adept at accumulating riches that can be taken with us into the next life.

The idea of downscaling takes a while to get used to. It's like Mike Tyson being told that the heavyweight boxing crown doesn't entitle him to any woman he wants, and that he still has to live by the rules protecting other people. When a person is used to privilege, he or she doesn't adjust easily to limitations.

Most of the world's people outside North America hold the opinion that we Americans manifest an attitude of entitlement. They sense we feel we deserve the abundance we have. Maybe they're right. Perhaps that's why the concept of downscaling seems so strange to us.

The truth is that for some, downscaling is both timely and necessary, because they're living beyond their means. They consistently spend more than they take in. So in their case, scaling down involves learning how to live within the confines of what they earn, and in time even setting aside some funds for unexpected expenses.

But downscaling is more than that. It's getting in the habit of saying, "I could buy it, but I won't." This is not easy for people who live in a society where *shop* is no longer primarily a noun but a verb. Early Americans used to go to a shop to buy what they needed. They gave the owner a request, and he went to the back room to get the tool, the bolt of material, or whatever their necessities required.

Our world changed when shop owners discovered the advantages of letting their patrons see everything that was available in the back room. When that happened, suddenly customers wanted more than the items on their lists. So over time more and more merchandise from the storeroom was brought forward and put on display. Today in North America we can see practically all the goods from all the back rooms of the world. The array is truly mind-boggling. Just to go to look at it is a fun experience—to shop (the verb). And the more we see when browsing, the harder it is for us to say no, to limit our purchases to items on a list of needs.

Downscaling means more than just cutting back. It also involves learning to be satisfied. Hebrews 13:5 reads, "Be content with what you have." Can you be content with where you live even if it never rivals the homes pictured in *House Beautiful?* Can you be thankful for a reliable car even though it doesn't look as spectacular as the one in the commercial? Downscaling is finding that a proper contentment level can be reached if we work at it. We don't have to keep up with the Joneses.

Downscaling says, "We're satisfied; we really are. What we have may not be adequate for somebody else, but for us it's fine. We can do without a second house, even though we could afford it now. We don't really need to put more in savings, or get a membership in that organization. But you go ahead and enjoy it if you want."

Downscaling. I'm not trying to give the exact definition, I'm just expanding the concept of this survival skill.

Investing in Heavenly Treasures

Based on what Jesus talked about, I would say that downscaling also necessitates investing more in heavenly treasures than in earthly ones. That's important to understand. We won't be able to take anything into the next world that chips or peels or rusts or breaks or gets moth holes in it or gets stolen. So it's best to concentrate on laying up for ourselves treasures that will transfer into the world that's yet to be (Matt. 6:19-26).

Recently I was speaking for a week at the Moody Keswick Bible Conference in St. Petersburg, Florida and I met a number of believers in their late sixties and early seventies. They weren't guests, although they easily could have been. These folks had the resources to take a luxurious cruise if they wanted, or stay for a while at a five-star hotel. But they were working as *volunteer* staff for thirteen weeks during the Bible conference season, doing maintenance work, helping with food service, ushering at meetings, leading activities with the guests. They were storing up treasures they could take with them to the next world. And in so doing they were helping me understand the eternal value of downscaling.

Grover's Corners, New Hampshire is the setting for Thornton Wilder's Pulitzer Prize-winning play, *Our Town.* When the audience enters the theatre, the stage is bare. As late arrivals are seated, the stage manager puts in place a few chairs, tables, and a bench. Other than this, there is no scenery on stage.

"The First Act shows a day in our town," the stage manager explains as the play starts. "The day is May 7, 1901. The time is just before dawn." Then we hear a rooster crowing in the background as the lone figure onstage proceeds to explain how the town is laid out. "Over there is the Congregational Church; across the street's the Presbyterian. Methodist and Unitarian are over there. Baptist is down in the holla' by the river."

When Act Two begins, it's 1904. The stage manager catches us up on all that's happened in the thousand days which have elapsed. We also watch a delightful romance unfold between young George Gibbs, the son of the busy town doctor, and Emily, who lives in the house next door. Her dad is Editor Webb, who prints the Grover's Corners *Sentinel.* The wedding ceremony of George and Emily concludes this act.

"Gradual changes in Grover's Corners," says the stage manager as the Third Act starts. Now it's 1913. "Horses are getting rarer. Farmers coming into town in Fords. Everybody locks their house doors now at night. Ain't been any burglars in town yet, but everybody's heard about 'em."

The mood of this act is different. That's because the young wife, Emily, a character we've grown quite fond of, has died in childbirth. Now as Wilder portrays this last of three days in the life of a small town, he shows what he thinks we should value about our lives in America.

During the grave-side ceremony, Emily symbolically walks away from the mourning party to join those of the town who have died and are buried. In one corner of the stage they sit almost motionless on chairs arranged in neat rows, like gravestones in a cemetery.

Emily is confused as she talks with these people she once knew. It's obvious she still has deep feelings toward the loved ones she has left behind. As she sits down in her new surroundings, she decides she wants to go back. "Why, just then for a moment I was thinking about . . . about the farm . . . and for a minute I was there, and my baby was on my lap plain as day. . . . I can go back there and live all those days over again . . . why not?"

But her mother-in-law, Mother Gibbs, who died three years earlier, responds, "All I can say is, Emily, don't." And others who are dead advise the same thing, "Emily, don't. It's not what you think it'd be."

In spite of their warnings, Emily returns to relive some of her former existence. She chooses to once again watch her twelfth birthday, only to discover that people were so busy with life they really didn't see each other. At one point she calls out, "Oh, Mama, just look at me one minute as though you really saw me." Again, "It goes so fast. We don't have time to look at one another."

Emily questions the stage manager, "Do any human beings ever realize life while they live it? — every, every minute?"

"No," is the response. Then after a long pause, "The saints and poets, maybe — they do some."

As I indicated earlier, Thornton Wilder calls for no scenery in his play and uses very few props. Most material things are left to the imagination of the audience. If I'm correct, he's implying that we should concentrate on the people in the play and on how they relate to one another. That's what he sees as important.

To my knowledge, Wilder wasn't a Christian. But his message in *Our Town* is one I believe the Lord affirms. Human beings are all too prone to get taken up with the sets and the props, and to totally miss what's important — until it's too late.

When I read this play or see it performed on stage, I feel uneasy. I'm too much like busy Dr. Gibbs, or like Emily's father, Editor Webb, with his daily deadlines to meet. And I fear that before I know it, someone very important to me will be gone.

Setting Priorities

Possibly that's one reason downscaling is emerging as an attractive discipline for me to explore. It's an opportunity to set priorities and then make sure that what's most important in life gets the emphasis it should.

A logical area in which to begin setting priorities is material things. We certainly don't want to end up like the wealthy farmer God called a fool. The final day of his life he was still planning for his bigger and better barns, chasing treasures on earth rather than laying up for himself some riches in heaven.

When Paul wrote his first letter to Timothy, he captured what we too would do well to understand. In chapter 6, verses 17-19, Paul says:

> Command those who are rich in this present world not to be arrogant nor to put their hope in wealth, which is so uncertain, but to put their hope in God, who richly provides us with everything for our enjoyment. Command them to do good, to be rich in good deeds, and to be generous and willing to share. In this way they will lay up treasure for themselves as a firm foundation for the coming age, so that they may take hold of the life that is truly life.

A second downscaling front to keep an eye on is time. Let's not discover too late that being busy usually means that we don't really see people. We need to determine what time-wasters we can eliminate, and what wise ways to use time we can incorporate more and more into our normal routine.

I'm still struggling here. I'm a recovering workaholic who still takes on more responsibilities than he should. I certainly don't waste time. But that doesn't mean I invest my time in the wisest possible ways. I know some cutting back on projects will be necessary, some delegating, some letting go of things, and I'm nervous about how all that's going to work out.

I've never been a spendthrift. Material things are not what drive me. That aspect of downscaling will come more easily for me. But I'm aware that as my means have grown, my spending has risen right alongside of it. And I haven't saved as I should, or set aside a proper amount for retirement. So financial downscaling won't be an automatic success. I do feel the Lord is saying to me that this is a direction in which I need to move.

What is this focus on downscaling saying to you?

• Is there an attraction to getting off the treadmill and really starting to notice the people you live with and say you love?

• What about shifting your emphasis from accumulating goods here on earth to actively laying up for yourself treasures in heaven?

• Can you challenge the idea of bigger and better by discovering contentedness in the Lord's daily provision for your needs?

• Could you find that there is as much joy in giving things away as you thought you felt while you were accumulating them?

• Might you experience a new freedom by learning to live more simply?

• Could beginning to say, "I was going to buy that, but now I won't," bring you immediate joy as well as long-range satisfaction?

• Is downscaling an appropriate survival skill for you to work on in this changing decade of the '90s?

Christ often challenged the people He loved to consider downscaling. Mark 10 tells the story of the rich young ruler. Verse 21 reads, "Jesus looked at him and loved him." Then, the account goes on, our Lord told this young man to sell all he had, give the proceeds to the poor, and follow Him. If the man did that, Jesus said, he would have treasure in heaven. Christ's advice was motivated by compassion and love.

If you sense that Jesus has a similar word for you, and you're wondering if He knows what He's asking, recall these incredible words from Philippians 2 about His own downscaling: "Being in very nature God ... [He] made Himself nothing, taking the very nature of a servant. ... He humbled Himself and became obedient to death—even death on a cross!" (vv. 6-8)

That quickly puts things in perspective, doesn't it?

FOR DISCUSSION AND REFLECTION

1.   What aspects of downscaling seem most attractive to you? Why?

2.   What don't you like about the concept of down-scaling? Why?

3.   Why do you think Jesus said it was hard for a rich man to enter the kingdom of God?

4.   Name several ways you could store up for yourself treasures in heaven, in addition to what you already have been doing.

5.   Which is the biggest problem for you: cutting back on your schedule or cutting back on your spending?

6.   Is it accurate to call downscaling a survival skill? Why or why not?

READINGS

My soul was drying up. I was tormented by the knowledge I carried about inside my heart and head. Others had not seen what I had seen in Asia, and I could not forget the people I had left behind. I was haunted by memories of millions of lost souls in North India, and the suffering, forgotten little band of native missionaries I knew was still trying to reach them for God.

So for two years, my heart had hardened. I had not shed a tear for them. In fact, I could not shed a tear for anyone or anything. Then as I prayed and evaluated my life in the light of eternity, it all changed. I let go of one materialistic thing after another—to surrender my ambitions and plans for future ministry in the safety and security of America.

During two weeks of prayer, I made a deliberate decision to put it all on the altar and let God once again have total control of my life. Suddenly, a dam of tears broke within, and I could once more weep and feel the love of Christ for lost souls.

My life-style was up for grabs. Everything and every action were tested against the literal teaching of Scripture. I decided that I would lay up no treasure for myself on this earth. I made a definite choice to put the kingdom of God first and trust Him to "add all these things unto me."

Our life-style became simpler. My new car was the first thing to go. Insurance policies, savings accounts, credit cards, most of my clothes—everything that could be was sold off so the money could be sent to needy native brethren.

But we never missed a thing. It was such a joy to move in the flow of the Holy Spirit again. Suddenly we were free. We had wings like eagles to soar above our bondage to these material playthings. In one stroke, we as a family were again having a significant impact on a lost and dying world. We knew that we were exercising the mind of Christ about these things, and we began trusting our Father to provide for our needs.

A Changed Life-style

In fact, finding new ways to save money for missions became a game at our house. I started washing with generic soap instead of fancy brand names. Magazine subscriptions and wasted hours before the television disappeared from our lives as did the time I once spent matching the color combinations of my wardrobe.

I had no regrets. we were no longer seeking to improve our life-style, worrying about investment portfolios, saving for a rainy day—and all the other nonsense which cripples and destroys the lives of so many Christians in this country.

The Road to Reality, K.P. Yohannan, Creation House, pages 144–145.

● ● ●

Finally, the saints among us are often found in surprising places. They give the lie to the assumption that only the well-placed and powerful can make a difference. For example, women yield a disproportionate percentage of saints among us (15 percent of women are saints, as opposed to 11 percent of men). Blacks are twice as likely as whites to be saints among us. Saints are slightly more likely to be found in the South or earn under $25,000 each year. The saints are almost twice as likely to be found among those who did not graduate from high school as among those with college degrees. For the most part, the faith of the saints reveals a simple goodness. They remind us of Jesus' words that in the transformed values of the kingdom the ones that the present world considers the last shall be first. Many come from what society considers the least recognized and least powerful group: the nonwhite, female poor. When we think about the ones who change the course of history, we tend to include the powerful and wealthy, the presidents and their staffs. We think of those with position and education, with leverage and economic advantage. But the saints among us may matter far more. They are making a contribution to society too little recognized, too quickly overlooked.

It is true that the saints we found do not often stride down our government's corridors of power, but their influence, because of its dailyness, is consistent. Many lack formal theological training, but have fashioned a workable faith that works in the push and pull of the businesses, factories, and neighborhoods they inhabit. They also stand close enough to daily need to be humble, not proud. If they stopped to think about it, they could resonate with the apostle Paul's admonishment in 1 Corinthians: "Think of what you were when you were called. Not many of you were wise by human standards; not many were influential; not many were of noble birth. But God chose the foolish things of the world to shame the wise. . . . He chose the lowly things of this world . . . so that no one may boast before him" (1 Cor. 1:26-29, NIV). For all their simplicity, the saints among us leave a mark in our communities and in our lives.

The Saints Among Us, George H. Gallup, Jr. and Timothy Jones, Morehouse Publishing, pages 44–45.

● ● ●

One of the most profound effects of inward simplicity is the rise of an amazing spirit of contentment. Gone is the need to strain and pull to get ahead. In rushes a glorious indifference to position, status, or possession. Living out of this wonderful Center causes all other concerns to fade into insignificance. So utterly immersed was St. Paul in this reality that from a Roman prison he could write, "I have learned, in whatever state I am, to be content" (Phil. 4:11). To be abased or to abound was a matter of indifference to him. Plenty and hunger, abundance and want were immaterial to this little Jew with the Titan soul. "I can do all things through Christ who strengthens me," he said, and so he lived (Phil. 4:13, NKJV).

How cleverly Paul turned the tables on all those who taught that "godliness is a means of gain" by replying that "there is great gain in godliness with contentment" (1 Tim. 6:5, 6). He saw that the problem with material gain is its inability to bring contentment. John D. Rockefeller was once asked how much money it would take to be really satisfied.

He answered, "Just a little bit more!" And that is precisely our problem — it always takes a little more....

But the wonderful thing about simplicity is its ability to give us contentment. Do you understand what a freedom this is? To live in contentment means we can opt out of the status race and the maddening pace that is its necessary partner. We can shout, "No!" to the insanity which chants, "More, more, more!..."

I still remember the day this reality struck me with unusual force. I was passing by some very expensive homes, and began pondering our perennial tendency to want something bigger, better, and more plush. At the same time, I was monitoring the rise of covetousness in my spirit as I admired those homes. I carried on a little inward dialogue. Was it possible, I wondered, to come to the place where you do not desire more house even if you can afford it? Couldn't you decide on a particular economic livability and rest contented with that, even if your income exceeded it considerably? The response was swift: "Oh yes! It is not necessary to always crave more. You *can* live contented with what you have, with no further desire to accumulate more." I'm quite sure I have not attained this holy contentment, but from time to time I have known a measure of its liberating graces and have found it a wonderful resting place.

Think of the misery that comes into our lives by our restless gnawing greed. We plunge ourselves into enormous debt and then take two and three jobs to stay afloat. We uproot our families with unnecessary moves just so we can have a more prestigious house. We grasp and grab and never have enough. And most destructive of all, our flashy cars and sports spectaculars and backyard pools have a way of crowding out much interest in civil rights or inner city poverty or the starved masses of India. Greed has a way of severing the cords of compassion. How clearly the Apostle Paul saw this when he warned that our lust for wealth causes us to fall into "many senseless and hurtful desires that plunge men into ruin and destruction" (1 Tim. 6:9).

Freedom of Simplicity, Richard J. Foster, Harper & Row, pages 87–88.

● ● ●

A Journey Toward Simplicity:
Walter and Virginia Hearn

A few years ago we sensed that God wanted us to do something different with our lives, but we didn't realize how radical a change it would be.

The competitive professional rat race left us little time to think and write. We had seen what happens to families when a husband spends himself and all his time at a demanding job. Even with two children to support and Ginny's elderly mother to care for, we felt there must be another way for us. We were willing to trust God and "count the cost" of trying something different, some way of working together in a new kind of life. So we kept careful records and deliberately pared our cost of living down to half our income. By saving the other half, each year on the payroll "bought" us a year to experiment. We stayed two years, then took the plunge and moved to Berkeley.

Our family enterprise (writing and editing) doesn't support us yet, but we seldom panic. God has been teaching us how much we can do without. He has reinforced our basic decision in various ways, and provided bits of income to keep us in "bread" and hope. We think he intends for us to survive. So now we have made another decision: Whenever we do begin to earn more money, we are resolved not to let our "standard of living" rise along with our income. We are beginning to feel liberated.

Cutting down doesn't come easy in our society. Possessions have become the measure of everything, even of spiritual worth, and commercial interests control or dominate most channels of communication. What we have done goes against the American grain.

We think that deliberately lowering our standard of living in obedience to God is part of what Jesus meant by being "poor in spirit." The amazing thing is that the quality of our life seems higher than before.

Of course, we have to beware of the reverse snobbery of spiritual one-up-manship. No matter how little one learns to live on, even *that* comes at the expense of someone else. What each of us has is a gift, no matter how we stand financially. Greed tempts the poor as well as the rich. Christians need not put down people who are wealthy, wasteful, extravagant or stingy, as long as we don't follow their ways. God is their judge, and ours. We ought rather to put our energy into being examples of a better way, just as Jesus Christ is ours. Each person must live his or her own life as God leads them. We don't want to overgeneralize from our experience. Our Father seems to love variety.

Living More Simply, edited by Ronald J. Sider, InterVarsity Press, pages 73–75.

● ● ●

Even with a good budget, the ends never seem to meet. But that's the point! Budgets aren't for making ends meet. Money isn't an end. Budgets are for making *means* fall into line! The ends we want are what Paul calls the fruits of the Spirit: "love, joy, peace, patience, kindness, goodness, faithfulness, gentleness, self-control" (Gal. 5:22-23). A budget won't buy them, but governing our money wisely may free us to find them.

Let's begin with what we'll give away. If you wait until you have paid for everything else and then start looking for leftovers to share, there won't be any. But if you start with your gifts, by an amazing miracle you will almost always find that there is enough left over to meet the necessities. (I didn't believe that either until I tried it on a dare with myself, but it does work.) Okay, what percentage of my money shall I give? All Christians know the word *tithe*, which simply means 10 percent. But to some the word has a hateful sound. Let's face it, a tithe from one person is harder than a tithe from another. If you made three thousand dollars a year (which is *thirty* times as much as as most of the world's people make!) a tithe of three hundred dollars might mean shoes or beans for children who otherwise might go hungry or barefoot. But if you made $300,000.00 a year you could probably squeak by fairly well on the $270,000.00 left over after the tithe. In fact, tax-wise, you would be better off to increase your giving to charitable causes. So we just can't say: Make it an automatic 10 percent and let it go. What do you do then? Why not take a hard look at what you are actually giving now. What is it? Two percent of your gross income? Five percent? You know a lot of us got into the habit of putting a quarter into the plate when our parents gave it to us as children, and we're still operating at that level. Now set yourself a goal of increasing it a little (maybe one or two percentage points a year) until you get to a place that you honestly consider a sacrificial level. Don't stop at 10 percent. I know a family that puts aside *30* percent of their income into a special bank account each month. At the end of the month, they take pleasure in writing a check for 10 percent to their church, another 10 percent to regular causes in their community, and (here's the best part), they save the third portion to build up interest until something really special comes along. Then they have a family council and decide how to spend it. Can you imagine how much more fun it is to decide what to do with a surplus than to have the usual squabble over what to trim?

But never mind about what the Joneses are doing. You and I have to establish our own budgets, not somebody else's. And no simple formula will work. The tithe means 10 percent. But is that 10 percent to the church, or 10 percent to all charitable causes? And do I take it off before or after income taxes? The answer is none of these things. That figure of 10 percent which used to be a legal obligation on the ancient Hebrews, is still a good starting point for Christian giving, but it isn't the end we seek. To give the whole tithe to the church, after taxes would merely be a duty fulfilled and no grounds for glory (see Luke 17:10). We can't stop there. Like the rich young man, we have to go the whole way (Mark 10:21).

Traveling Light, Pat McGeachy, Abingdon Press, pages 87–89.

CHAPTER TWO
OFF-LOADING STRESS

A professional actor I know once invited me to see the play *1776*. He had the role of Thomas Jefferson in this particular production.

The plot of *1776* actually centers around John Adams, as he attempts to get the Second Continental Congress in Philadelphia to act decisively and declare independence from England. The times call for change. But certain members of this congress are painfully slow to move. The representatives lack imagination or are even self-serving. As you watch you wonder how in the world they will emerge with a united spirit.

Adams, seeing the issues clearly, struggles to gather support for what he believes in so strongly. Even though no colonies have ever before broken away from a mother country, these men must seize the hour and vote for independence.

Unfortunately, John Dickenson from Pennsylvania gets a motion passed that in order to approve the declaration written by Thomas Jefferson of Virginia, the vote must be unanimous. All thirteen colonies must say yes. And it's obvious there's no way such agreement will ever be reached.

Emergency dispatches continue to arrive from General George Washington, who was made chief of the continental forces a year earlier. He's in New York where the British have just landed 25,000 crack troops. He writes that it's imperative that action be taken.

I'll never forget one scene in the play. It's the night of July 3, 1776. The hall is empty save for John Adams, who reviews the facts as he sees them. South Carolina and Pennsylvania are opposed to the motion for independence. Delaware is undecided. New York's representatives are awaiting further instructions. It looks hopeless.

Wrestling with a vision shared by only a few, Adams paces back and forth in the hall. We can feel the stress in his body as we watch. Suddenly he looks up and cries out dramatically into the void:

Is anybody there!
Does anybody care!
Does anybody see what I see!

I found that moment very moving. I was engrossed in the whole scenario: the magnitude of what was being decided, the frustration Adams must have felt, the rightness of the cause he believed in so strongly, and the anxiety as time was running out. It was all so real, I got caught up in the tension, forgetting momentarily that I knew what had to happen on the Fourth of July!

Stress in Changing Times
Times of change are always stressful. That's obviously true when a national resolution is in process. It's also the case when a country's basic values are later tested by an issue such as slavery—or, more recently, abortion.

Even in the personal realm, a change in circumstances, almost always adds an element of strain to life. For example, moving to a new location creates anxiety, as does losing a job or even taking on a new one. You might feel stress when you begin attending a different church, when you retire, or when you see rapid growth or steady decline in your business. Getting married, getting divorced, going for counseling to correct longstanding dysfunction, dealing with a serious illness in the family—all these situations add an element of stress. And the list could go on and on.

Stress seems to be a part of our American way of life. This is a fast-paced culture where changes come rapid-fire. So headaches are cared for with a couple of aspirin or Tylenol™ tablets. Chronic body symptoms can be suppressed with a swig of Pepto-Bismol™ or maybe a spoonful of Metamucil™.

Do you relate at all to that word *stress?* Some say, "Ignore the pressures, forget the deadlines, let someone else do what you're doing. So what if you kill yourself for that dream you hold so dear. The world will go right on."

And suddenly you feel like John Adams walking the floor all alone, reviewing the facts and sensing there is no hope. You reread the emergency fax that came in that afternoon: "It's imperative that you act now!" You're sure there's no way things could possibly work out the way they should, and that, unfortunately, this critical opportunity isn't going to come around again for a long time.

When change is accompanied by stress, it needs to be off-loaded daily onto Christ. Instead of venting feelings late at night in a room where no one can see you, as a Christian, learn how to "cast all your anxiety on Him because He cares for you." That's a promise from 1 Peter 5:7. Jesus really does care.

Most people know what Scripture teaches, but they don't always know how to put it into practice. This brief prayer should help you begin to off-load your stress.

Father,
You are God, even in stress-filled times. On my own I could feel overwhelmed, but Scripture tells me You care about every detail of my life.

Right now, the stress I feel most intensely is (and then you fill in the blank):

- My car doesn't work, God, and You know I don't have the money to fix it.
- The deadline on this report is only a week away. Without help I'll never get it done on time.
- I've had bouts with skin cancer for the last several years, Lord. Now it seems as though there's a growth in my breast and I'm afraid even to go to the doctor.
- We were on top of everything, God. Then our computer system crashed in the storm, and I'm stunned! I don't know where to start repairing the damage.
- I have to speak at the banquet in three days and I still

have no clue as to what to say.
- The taxes are due and I have nothing to pay them.
- My boss is unreasonable in his expectations. The only way I can make it is to work on weekends. I'm sorry, God.
- My dad's been sick so we've moved him to our house. Now the extra responsibility is making me extremely nervous. How will I handle taking care of the kids and him too?
- I'll never pass the exam. I got way behind on studying because of my night job.
- Our marriage is going from bad to worse. We don't seem to be able to communicate anymore.
- I took on too much with this new church responsibility. I've never done anything this extensive before, and I'm having real trouble getting on top of it.

With these few examples, I may not have identified an area where you feel pressure. So it's important that you fill in the blank each day with the specific stress you feel. The prayer then continues.

Show me steps I can take, and give me the courage to take them.

In the quiet of prayer, I find that as I wait on the Lord, in other words, as I stop talking momentarily, He brings to mind specific steps I can take. He gives me divine direction for the given day! Then I need to ask for courage to take these steps.

I admit sometimes I pray this prayer when I'm in the car driving to work. If need be, the Lord can make His will known even in the midst of morning traffic.

Then I love this final line:

Calm my spirit, Lord, as I trust You to bring good in this situation. Amen.

A Calm Spirit
A calm spirit even in the midst of tension has to be a sign of the Lord's miracle-presence. The Apostle Paul writes to the

Philippians, "Do not be anxious about anything, but in every-thing, by prayer and petition, with thanksgiving, present your requests to God. [Now note this.] And the peace of God, which transcends all understanding, will guard your hearts and your minds in Christ Jesus" (Phil. 4:6-7).

When our four children were growing up, they would get into the normal squabbles that kids in the same family have. So Karen would make them sit on the church pew which serves as a couch in our living room. What they had to do was say, "Calm my spirit, calm my spirit," until it was obvious their spirits had been calmed. This was in lieu of discipline of another sort.

I can still see two little boys—or a brother and sister—sitting on that pew, swinging their legs back and forth, still upset, repeating, "Calm my spirit, calm my spirit, calm my spirit, calm my spirit." Actually, the technique worked more often than you might imagine.

While you're getting used to praying, "Calm my spirit," you may feel a little like one of my young children sitting on our church pew. At first you want to get back into what's going on and resolve things. You say the words "Calm my spirit," but your mind and body will still be racing.

But don't count this prayer out until you've tried it for a while. I believe you'll discover it's far more effective than you imagined possible. And it sure beats shouting your frustration—as John Adams did in *1776*—to an empty room.

Do you remember *The Sound of Music* as it unfolds on the big screen? Major changes are taking place in Austria. The Nazis have taken over the country, and we watch how this affects the von Trapp family. Maybe you recall the huge flag with the German swastika being draped from the front balcony of the family mansion. That scene graphically symbolizes what's happening.

Maria, played by Julie Andrews, may not have been an asset to the abbey where she was a postulant. But she has found her true calling in marrying Captain von Trapp—and becoming stepmother to his seven children. Maria proves her worth time and time again, and eventually the entire family escapes from Austria and Nazi dominion.

As good as this musical is, much of the advice given about dealing with the stress of changing times is somewhat surface. For example, I doubt that remembering your favorite things will keep you from feeling badly when the dog bites or the bee stings.

Let's look at some lines of a song written at another time during an earlier day of national and personal tension.

> The Lord is my light and my salvation—
>   whom shall I fear?
> The Lord is the stronghold of my life—
>   of whom shall I be afraid? ...
>
> Though an army besiege me,
>   my heart will not fear;
> though war break out against me,
>   even then will I be confident.
>
> Hear my voice when I call, O Lord. ...
> My heart says of You, "Seek His face!"
>   Your face, Lord, I will seek. ...
>
> Be strong and take heart
>   and wait for the Lord (Ps. 27:1-3, 7-8, 14).

David's advice sounds a bit more substantive. During times of extreme stress, his practice was to seek the Lord.

When your anxiety level rises, which of these two approaches seems more characteristic of you? Too many Christians know in their heads that they should first talk with their Father in heaven. But they never seem to actually get around to it. They don't say, as David did, "Hear my voice when I call, O Lord; be merciful to me and answer me" (v. 7). Instead, they practice a homegrown method, concentrating first on talking their problems out with everyone else they can find.

Stress in the '90s
The '90s could be years of stress for many of us. The changes in our culture have hardly been all for the good. And

because stress can kill a person, a key survival skill is knowing how to successfully off-load it.

"Hold on. My worries are hardly on as grand a scale as you've been talking about. My kids aren't into singing together von Trapp style, and we're not trying to figure out how to escape over the Alps. The facts are that: (1) We don't own a mansion for some enemy to hang his big flag on, and (2) I don't look much like Julie Andrews (or Christopher Plummer). We're just simple people trying to figure out how to buy the kids clothes for school and whether we'll have enough cash for groceries next week. Can you relate to that? Our problems aren't spectacular, but they're very real to us."

My answer is that your stress and my stress are probably not the same. But apparently Jesus knew a lot of people in your position. He says in Matthew 6:

> Therefore I tell you, do not worry about your life, what you will eat or drink; or about your body, what you will wear. . . . Look at the birds of the air; they do not sow or reap or store away in barns, and yet your Heavenly Father feeds them. Are you not much more valuable than they? [The implication is that obviously you are!] . . . Therefore do not worry about tomorrow, for tomorrow will worry about itself. Each day has enough trouble of its own (vv. 25-26, 34).

Our Lord is saying two things here. First, He is assuring us that God is concerned about matters as basic as food and clothing. In the model prayer Jesus taught His disciples, He instructed them to pray, "Lord, give us this day our daily bread." Second, Christ is telling us we shouldn't pick up tomorrow's problems prematurely. So the off-loading of stress I'm talking about is not meant to be done on a weekly basis, but every day. That's important.

Don't get too far ahead in your stress-related prayers. To pray too far into the future almost discourages faith. It's like saying, "I assume little is going to change for the good in the next month, Lord." Instead, focus your prayers more on the immediate, on the day at hand. "Right now the stress I feel most intensely is _____ . Jesus, You said tomorrow will worry about itself. So I'm only talking to You about the 'right now' of my life."

Then believe that God will give your "today prayer" the kind of attention you feel it deserves. After all, that's the bottom line. You want to know if this works, right? Will this pill relieve my tension, take away the headache, soothe the nervous stomach? Are the commercials true? They claim all these products perform minor miracles. Do they really? Simply remembering my favorite things may sound good in a song, but in real life, when I'm shaking in fear, that advice leaves a lot to be desired.

Here we're talking about "goods" from the religious counter. And you may be thinking, "To be honest, sometimes when I hear the 'ad copy' it's as if the church doesn't know that stress is tearing people up. We're talking survival and you ministers often promote products as if nobody's stressed out."

Not so! I'm pushing this new Off-loading Stress Prayer because I know it works wonders!

**Father,
You are God, even in stress-filled times.**

That's true. Stress is not something new to Him. He experienced it firsthand when He came to earth in the person of His Son. Witnesses say Jesus felt tension so great that He sweat drops of blood.

**On my own I could feel overwhelmed,
But Scripture tells me You care about every detail
of my life.**

That's valid. He's concerned about all our needs: for necessities, health, guidance, support, protection—you name it!

**Right now, the stress I feel most intensely is
_____ (complete the sentence).**

Right now—that's in line with what Jesus said about each day having enough trouble of its own. Don't start worrying today about tomorrow. Instead, tell God the "right now" stress you feel most intensely. This is the off-loading part, when you tell the Lord what it is you want help with. "I need You today, God, to carry this load along with me."

Show me steps I can take, and give me the courage to take them.

"You don't need to talk out loud, Lord: just sort of whisper Your thoughts in my heart. Maybe I should take a step of faith. Perhaps I need to ask forgiveness of someone. Possibly I need to fast, or by faith to start acting as if You've lifted the burden already, even though at the moment circumstances don't bear this out."

Calm my spirit, Lord, as I trust You to bring good in this situation.

Yes, it's a good prayer product. It walks you down the path you're supposed to follow if you want relief. It's spiritual medicine to be taken every day, preferably in the morning. If this prayer becomes habit-forming, that's only to your benefit, because all the side effects are good.

Then don't forget to say *Amen.* That means, "I'm assuming You're giving Your attention to this, Lord."

Use this prayer for several weeks and the life change will be such that you'll swear the ingredients are miraculous. And they are!

FOR DISCUSSION AND REFLECTION

1.   On a scale of 1 to 10 (10 being best), evaluate how skilled you are at handling stress. Explain the reason for the number you chose.

2.   What stressful situation is uppermost in your mind right now?

3.   Do you plan to make use of the prayer in this chapter? Why or why not?

4.   How does prayerfully asking God to show you steps you can take to off-load your stress differ from just thinking about what to do on your own?

5.   Tell about a time you believe God answered your prayer and helped you during a time of stress.

6.   Is it appropriate for you to think of learning to off-load stress as a skill you need to survive? Why or why not?

READINGS

The following table shows the ten situations most often selected by married men, married women, and single mothers as being stressful in their families

Top Stresses in Order of Priority

Total Group
1. Economics/finances/budgeting
2. Children's behavior/discipline/sibling fighting
3. Insufficient couple time
4. Lack of shared responsibility in the family
5. Communicating with children
6. Insufficient "me" time
7. Guilt for not accomplishing more
8. Spousal relationship (communication, friendship, sex)
9. Insufficient family playtime
10. Overscheduled family calendar

Female Married
1. Economics/finances/budgeting
2. Lack of shared responsibility in the family
3. Insufficient couple time
4. Children's behavior/discipline/sibling fighting
5. Housekeeping standards
6. Insufficient "me" time
7. Guilt for not accomplishing more
8. Insufficient family playtime
9. Spousal relationship (communication, friendship, sex)
10. Self-image/self-esteem/feelings of unattractiveness

Male Married
1. Economics/finances/budgeting
2. Insufficient couple time
3. Communicating with children
4. Children's behavior/discipline/sibling fighting

5. Spousal relationship (communication, friendship, sex)
6. Overscheduled family calendar
7. Insufficient "me" time
8. Unhappiness with work situation
9. Insufficient family playtime
10. Television

Single Mothers
1. Economics/finances/budgeting
2. Guilt for not accomplishing more
3. Insufficient "me" time
4. Self-image/self-esteem/feelings of unattractiveness
5. Children's behavior/discipline/sibling fighting
6. Unhappiness with work situation
7. Housekeeping standards
8. Communicating with children
9. Insufficient family playtime
10. Lack of shared responsibility in the family

Stress and the Healthy Family, Dolores Curran, Winston Press, pages 20–21.

● ● ●

It was at this point that Bruce's counseling began to take a strong positive turn. Through diet, exercise, and proper rest, he began to recover physically from the debilitating effects of stress that, if left unchecked, could have literally killed him.

Emotionally, he became far healthier as he learned to deal with anger rather than stuff it away, as had been his pattern in the past. At the suggestion of his counselor, Bruce developed a network of men who became his close friends, his confidants, and a valued resource for sharing emotions such as anger, fear, or discouragement. Bruce also learned new and effective interpersonal communications techniques, which strengthened his relationship with his wife and his children. That in turn had a positive effect on his son, who was undergoing treatment for his drug and alcohol problem.

Spiritually, Bruce was able to move from a driven, legalistic approach to his faith to the point where he, in his own words,

"Actually began to enjoy God for the first time in my life. I'd always viewed God like my dad—cold, isolated, ready to 'lay it on me' whenever I slipped up in the least possible way. Now I realize just how far off base that view of God was."

In his final session, we talked with Bruce about two important factors in his life: balance and serenity. After we discussed the competing demands of work, home, self, and others, Bruce pledged to continue to seek balance—and to request feedback from his wife as well as his new network of friends regarding any new areas of imbalance that might crop [up] in the future.

Toward the end of the session we contrasted the serenity prayer,

God grant me the serenity
To accept the things I cannot change,
The courage to change the things I can,
And the wisdom to know the difference.

with the workaholic's prayer we had talked about earlier:

Lord, help me get everything done.
Now, please, and in order.

With the insight he had gained during the previous weeks, Bruce was able to laugh at the difference between those two approaches to spirituality. And it was evident to us as we concluded the interview that, although Bruce had come to us reflecting the workaholic's prayer, he was leaving with the perspective of the serenity prayer.

We've been extremely gratified to see literally hundreds of men and women like Bruce achieve balance and serenity as they've brought the stress factor in their lives under control.

The Stress Factor, Frank Minirth and Paul Meier, Northfield Publishing, pages 175–176.

● ● ●

Our generation consumes huge quantities of sedatives, barbiturates, and other tranquilizers in mute testimony to its haunting anxieties. . . . Before our age of so-called miracle medicines a noted Bible commentator translated the Isaian reference to "the Prince of Peace" to read "the Tranquilizer." Jesus offered his disciples peace such as he knew on the way to crucifixion—and it wasn't a prescription for Valium.

Carl Henry at His Best, Carl F.H. Henry, Questar Publications, page 106.

●   ●   ●

A few days after returning to Bristol from his few weeks in Germany, and at a time of great financial distress in the work, a letter reached him from a brother who had often before given money, as follows:

"Have you any *present* need for the Institution under your care? I know you do not *ask,* except indeed of Him whose work you are doing; but to *answer when asked* seems another thing, and a right thing. I have a reason for desiring to know the present state of your means towards the objects you are labouring to serve: viz., should you *not have* need, other departments of the Lord's work, or other people of the Lord, *may have* need. Kindly then inform me, and to what amount, i.e. what amount you at this present time need or can profitably lay out."

To most men, even those who carry on a work of faith and prayer, such a letter would have been at least a temptation. But Mr. Müller did not waver. To announce even to an inquirer the exact needs of the work would, in his opinion, involve two serious risks:

1. It would turn his own eyes away from God to man;

2. It would turn the minds of saints away from dependence solely upon Him.

This man of God had staked everything upon one great experiment—he had set himself to prove that the prayer which *resorts to God only* will bring help in every crisis, even when the crisis is unknown to His people whom He uses as the means of relief and help.

At this time there remained in hand but twenty-seven pence ha'penny, in all, to meet the needs of hundreds of orphans. Nevertheless this was the reply to the letter:

"Whilst I thank you for your love, and whilst I agree with you that, in general, there is a difference between *asking for money* and *answering when asked,* nevertheless, in our case, I feel not at liberty to speak about the state of our funds, as the primary object of the work in my hands is to lead those who are weak in faith to see that there is *reality* in dealing with God *alone.*"

Consistently with his position, however, no sooner was the answer posted than the appeal went up to the Living God: "Lord, Thou knowest that, for Thy sake, I did not tell this brother about our need. Now, Lord, show afresh that there is *reality* in speaking to Thee only, about our need, and speak therefore to this brother so that he may help us." In answer, God moved this inquiring brother to send one hundred pounds, which came when *not one penny was in hand.*

The confidence of faith, long tried, had its increasing reward and was strengthened by experience. In July, 1845, Mr. Müller gave this testimony reviewing these very years of trial:

"Though for about seven years, our funds have been so exhausted that it has been comparatively a rare case that there have been means in hand to meet the necessities of the orphans *for three days* together, yet I have been only once tried in spirit, and that was on September 18, 1838, when for the first time the Lord seemed not to regard our prayer. But when He did send help at that time, and I saw that it was only for the trial of our faith, and not because He had forsaken the work, that we were brought so low, my soul was so strengthened and encouraged that I have not only not been allowed to distrust the Lord since that time, but I have not even been cast down when in the deepest poverty."

George Müller of Bristol, Arthur T. Pierson, The Baker and Taylor Company, pages 166–168.

● ● ●

Patrick of Ireland
(377–460)
Lorica, or The Breastplate

I arise today
Through a mighty strength, the invocation of the Trinity,
Through a belief in the Threeness,
Through confession of the Oneness
Of the Creator of creation.
I arise today
Through the strength of Christ's birth and His baptism,
Through the strength of His crucifixion and His burial,
Through the strength of His resurrection and His ascension,
Through the strength of His descent for the judgment of
doom.
I arise today
Through the strength of the love of cherubim,
In obedience of angels,
In service of archangels,
In the hope of resurrection to meet with reward,
In prayers of patriarchs,
In predictions of prophets,
In preachings of apostles,
In faiths of confessors,
In innocence of virgins,
In deeds of righteous men.
I arise today
Through the strength of heaven;
Light of the sun,
Radiance of the moon,
Splendor of fire,
Speed of lightning,
Swiftness of the wind,
Depth of the sea,
Stability of the earth,
Firmness of the rock.
I arise today
Through God's strength to pilot me;
God's might to uphold me,

God's wisdom to guide me,
God's eye to look before me,
God's ear to hear me,
God's word to speak for me,
God's hand to guard me,
God's way to lie before me,
God's shield to protect me,
God's hosts to save me
From snares of the devil,
From temptations of vices,
From every one who desires me ill,
Afar or anear,
Alone or in a multitude.
I summon today all these powers between me and evil,
Against every cruel merciless power that opposes my body
and soul,
Against incantations of false prophets,
Against black laws of pagandom,
Against false laws of heretics,
Against craft of idolatry,
Against spells of women and smiths and wizards,
Against every knowledge that corrupts man's body and soul.
Christ shield me today
Against poison, against burning,
Against drowning, against wounding,
So that reward may come to me in abundance.
Christ with me, Christ before me, Christ behind me,
Christ in me, Christ beneath me, Christ above me,
Christ on my right, Christ on my left,
Christ when I lie down, Christ when I sit down,
Christ when I arise,
Christ in the heart of every man who thinks of me,
Christ in the mouth of every man who speaks of me,
Christ in the eye that sees me,
Christ in the ear that hears me.
I arise today
Through a mighty strength, the invocation of the Trinity,
Through a belief in the Threeness,
Through a confession of the Oneness

Of the Creator of creation.

The Harper Book of Christian Poetry, Selected and Introduced by Anthony S. Mecatante, "Patrick of Ireland," Anonymous, pages 13–15.

CHAPTER THREE
COMBINING RESOURCES

Places in the Heart is a gentle, inspiring film starring Sally Field. The setting for the story is Waxahachie, Texas in 1935, during the Great Depression.

In the opening scene, Sheriff Spalding prays at dinner. His nine-year-old son, Frank, and younger daughter called Possum are seated at the table with their parents. "Father, please remind us in these hard times to be grateful for what we have been given."

He's just taken his first bite of fried chicken when there's a knock at the door. The report is that a young black is "drunk as a skunk" down by the railroad tracks, and he's got a gun. The sheriff leaves his dinner to make the arrest, never suspecting this is to be his last supper and his last prayer.

One of the things we all fear most is having to face the unexpected all alone. But that's the situation in which Edna Spalding finds herself.

Before long the local banker makes this new widow aware of just how precarious her financial position is. He encourages her to sell her house and modest acreage and to have the children raised by someone else. The rest of the film revolves around whether Edna will make it without having to succumb to the banker's suggestions.

Strictly on her own, she wouldn't have succeeded. But through a couple of unusual circumstances, Edna Spalding ends up with two boarders: Mr. Will, a blind World War I veteran; and Moze, an itinerant black handyman. For this group, it's come together or else. Each must contribute what he or she can or no one will survive—kids or adults. Edna Spalding makes this clear: The children will be sent to other

families, blind Mr. Will's future will be in an institution somewhere, and Moze will have to go back to begging door-to-door
for his meals.

Well, pull together they do. They survive a tornado plus
enough human greed and violence to discourage all but the
strongest of people. But this is an unusual group of five that's
formed—this small girl, this young boy, this widow, this black
itinerant worker, and this blind man. They become an indom-
itable team.

There are great sequences of blind Mr. Will cooking in the
kitchen so that the others, including both the kids, can pick
cotton in the fields; of Moze telling Mrs. Spalding how to
negotiate with the cotton buyer; and scenes showing how
Edna is the inspiration and determination behind all that gets
done.

After accomplishing the impossible by getting their cotton
harvested before anyone else (which results in a hundred-
dollar bonus), Mr. Will and Moze stay home while Mrs. Spalding and the children celebrate at a barn dance. Here there's
a touching scene where Frank, the young son, asks his mother to dance.

Back at the house, Mr. Will thinks he hears a noise outside. Moze doesn't hear anything, but to please Mr. Will he
goes outside to check the barn. There waiting for him are a
number of hooded figures of the Ku Klux Klan. When the
beating begins, Mr. Will hears it and feels for Sheriff Spalding's old pistol in the closet. What follows is an incredible
scene where a blind man with a handgun is able to stop the
beating of his black friend by Klan members.

In a way this action is typical of the film. None of the five
have a whole lot to give, but somehow the love of each for
the other, and the contribution of each to the whole, makes it
all work. Because of this mixture the simplest of lines—"Are
you OK?"—carries more power than you might expect.

Hard Times
No one should have to go through hard times by herself, or
by himself. Adults shouldn't have to. Certainly children
shouldn't! It's during tough times that we feel the need for

other's support most intensely.

Christians especially shouldn't be left in the position of having to face difficult days with little or no help. After all, we belong to what should be the most loving family in the world. God forgive us if that's true only doctrinally. With the vast resources available throughout the body of Christ, believers should never end up bearing their pain in isolation.

I don't believe they do, most of the time. I thrill to the many examples I hear about the family of God embracing those of its own who are hurting. These kinds of deeds include:

- Preparing meals
- Giving money
- Meeting transportation needs
- Offering temporary shelter
- Providing child care or foster homes
- Teaching English to immigrants
- Finding jobs for the unemployed
- Helping hurting people locate trained counselors

And the list goes on and on.

All around the world the church has been exemplary. To overlook that fact would mean we were incredibly naive. Time and again it's been the body of Christ that has compassionately asked, "Are you OK?" The truth is, "places in the heart" can easily be found among the people of God.

Through the centuries it's always been this way, even in the early days of the church. Acts 2:44-45, records that "all the believers were together and had everything in common. Selling their possessions and goods, they gave to anyone as he had need."

This is another unusual group, isn't it? It's much larger than a household of five. The church at this time already had several thousand members.

These verses come two chapters later, in Acts 4: "All the believers were one in heart and mind. No one claimed that any of his possessions was his own, but they shared everything they had. . . . There were no needy persons among them. For from time to time those who owned lands or houses sold them, brought the money from the sales and put it at the apostles' feet, and it was distributed to anyone as he had need" (vv. 32, 34-35).

I'm not asking that we in today's church match what's described here in Acts. The pressures we're under in our society don't even begin to compare to the tornado winds of change ripping through the lives of these New Testament people. The Son of God had recently been crucified. Fifty days later, the Holy Spirit had fallen on the church. The Jewish religious world was in a state of stubborn reaction, and the apostles were literally being beaten. It wouldn't be long before the Romans would destroy the temple and Jerusalem itself.

This passage in Acts just makes us aware that in the future we may have to come together even more than we have to date. We may need to love each other more, trust each other more, contribute more of what we have to give as individuals, if we want to survive.

I believe that when we learn to combine resources in God's family, we banish the fear of having to face the unexpected all alone. That may sound attractive to you, but the idea of combining resources may also be a bit scary.

Praise the Lord that on a larger scale, church leaders are setting a marvelous example in many communities. They're saying the power of the enemy will never be challenged unless we learn to stand together more in our towns and cities — Methodists, Baptists, Lutherans, Nazarenes, Presbyterians, Salvation Army, Assemblies of God, and so on. At the very minimum we can pray together.

Combining Resources

It's exciting to see this starting to happen in many settings. Sure, it means we'll be stretched in terms of trust. We may find ourselves joining forces with a person whose skin is a different color, or a minister we'd swear was spiritually blind, but love will find a way because we're talking about survival.

Wouldn't it be something if we could realize that on our own, none of us really have a whole lot to contribute, but that together we can become a powerful team, capable of bringing in a prize-winning harvest?

When I think about combining resources in the church, what I have in mind is not as radical as the Acts 2 and 4 passages where major properties are sold and the proceeds are distributed to those in need. Instead, I'm thinking of simple ideas, such as sharing outgrown children's clothing or maternity clothes.

I remember the clothes exchanges we had every so often in the church I pastored for ten years in inner-city Chicago. One Sunday after the morning service I saw someone who I thought was my wife, Karen, standing with her back to me, talking with someone. I walked over and put my arm around her, but it wasn't Karen! It was someone the same size wearing a dress of Karen's she had gotten in the clothes exchange the week before. No idea is perfect!

Why learn to combine resources? The first reason is that most of us are far too independent. We're part of a culture where people say, "I don't want to be a burden to anybody; I don't want to be dependent on somebody else; I don't like feeling obligated." Maybe that's OK in an era when everyone has adequate resources. But that's not true of this country as much anymore.

Here's another reason to learn to combine resources. Jesus said, "Do not turn away from the one who wants to borrow from you" (Matt. 5:42). Such a simple directive can be upsetting for someone who feels, "What's mine is mine, and you have no right to ask for it. That's true not just about big things like my car, that's how I feel about my books and my CDs and my videos and certainly my clothes. Just leave my stuff alone!"

Understanding that some people will have a strong reaction to this survival skill of combining resources, I'm trying to help you adjust to the idea very slowly. We'll start with little steps. In the long run you'll find them to be to your benefit.

Here's one small suggestion. You don't have to put off entertaining until you can do everything yourself. Call friends and say, "We could eat together Saturday night if you could fix a salad and dessert. I'll have the Dudley's bring bread and a vegetable. I'm taking care of the rest." That's combining resources.

Another idea would be to say, "Hey, I used to cut hair; you used to teach piano. Could we work out a deal so that our kids can become musicians—but not necessarily the long-haired kind?"

Combining resources is having more firewood than you need and offering some of it to a friend you know would enjoy it. And then maybe that person responds, "You're welcome to use the summer cottage some weekend."

Here's another example. "We have some minor plumbing problems. You're good at fixing things like that. And you've mentioned you need some pictures framed. I can do that. Why don't we just solve each other's problems?"

Combining resources could be as painless as exchanging magazines. "I'll give you my *Time* magazine a week after it comes. Why don't you let me see your copy of *Christianity Today?*"

Psalm 112:5 reads, "Good will come to him who is generous and lends freely." This psalm reinforces the truth that we don't have to fear the unexpected all alone. Verse 7 says that a righteous man (or woman) "will have no fear of bad news; his heart is steadfast, trusting in the Lord."

This passage also reminds us that there are always those within our ranks who are needy. In verse 9 we read that the blessed man, who is the focus of the psalm, "has scattered abroad his gifts to the poor." So another reason to learn to combine resources is that a lot of people are short of funds and need help. Many today are unemployed; some aren't paid much; others are facing unexpected major expenses. And there are always those who are unskilled in managing money. It doesn't really matter why a person is financially in need; those who are better off are called to show true compassion.

James, in his epistle, asks, "Suppose a brother or sister is without clothes and daily food. If one of you says to him, 'Go, I wish you well; keep warm and well fed,' but does nothing about his physical needs, what good is it?" (James 2:15-16) How many Christians have never in any substantive way helped a person in need?

Combining resources can mean, "I have money. You don't have a job right now, but you have skills. Help me with some yard jobs I've had trouble getting to, and I'll be more than happy to pay you."

In Isaiah 58:6-7 God asks, "Is not this the kind of fasting I have chosen? . . . To share your food with the hungry and to provide the poor wanderer with shelter—when you see the naked, to clothe him, and not to turn away from your own flesh and blood?" That last phrase, your own flesh and blood, could mean those in your extended family or the greater family of God.

Maybe combining resources means that a church in a more affluent neighborhood becomes partners with a low-income, inner-city outreach, and together they decide what each has to offer the other.

Or, it could be a congregation in America becoming a sister church to one in Russia or India or Bolivia, for example. They find out what each can give and receive, and then join forces to the glory of God.

One last reason to combine resources is that it is a marvelous testimony to the world. The film *Witness* starring Harrison Ford, portrays a glorious barn-raising sequence in Pennsylvania's Amish Country. The year is 1984 and early in the day we see the horse-drawn carriages converging on the building site. The men arrive with their carpentry tools strapped around their waists, and straw hats on their heads to protect them from the sun. The women immediately begin preparing food. To raise a barn in a day is a big job, but many hands doing many jobs will make it possible.

It's thrilling to watch as the first huge side frame is ready to be raised into place. Possibly as many as thirty men are involved with the ropes and pulleys. Before long it's up—careful, yes!—and standing.

Little children stop pounding on their play projects to take iced tea or lemonade to sweaty workers. The barn is slowly taking form. Soon the four side frames are standing and we see a structure that is large and impressive. This is no small project.

The team works with precision. Additional bracing and support pieces are fitted into place. The builders appear to be everywhere—working on the roof, hammering together framework and siding, fitting floors on the inside.

Now it's time to stop for lunch. And what a marvelous spread has been laid out by the women—chicken, potato salad, breads, garnishes. The men are hungry and they appreciate this feast.

Afternoon work includes teaching the older boys some basic building skills. The women quilt. The job is going to get done—that's obvious. Now there's time for more socializing. As the sun lowers, the carriages start leaving for home. And there against the sunset stands a magnificent barn that wasn't there when the day began. That's combining resources.

In spite of the unusual clothes and old-fashioned ways of the Amish, these people made an impression on me as a viewer. I said to myself, "There's something extremely good here. If a barn burns down, or a young couple gets married, these folks don't have to face the unexpected all alone. In turn, they will be loyal to the group and help when someone else has a need. This is the way it should be. And it is all done with such ease and grace and joy. How wonderful!"

As we learn from this illustration, combining resources can be attractive and attainable. We won't start by building a barn in one day, but it's good to know that a project that big is a possibility once we get adept at working together.

Maybe you'll begin by sharing a garden plot with someone. Try anything that challenges the mind-set that says, "Whatever I do, I have to own it or control it all by myself."

If I could guarantee that life will never blindside you, that a mate will never die, that disease will never attack your family, that a business will not fail, nor barns ever burn, we could probably forget about learning to combine resources.

But life isn't that predictable. We need to develop skills to help us survive changing times. And if we can learn to combine resources, we'll be assured that we won't have to face the unexpected all alone.

FOR DISCUSSION AND REFLECTION

1. Give an example of a way you have combined resources to the benefit of everyone involved.

2.   Do you know someone who would not have survived had it not been for the church's skill at combining resources? Describe the situation.

3.   What problems might surface when believers start combining resources?

4.   When Christians refuse to combine resources, what benefits do they miss?

5.   How does your church compare to the New Testament believers in the matter of combining resources? In what ways is your church doing well? How might it improve?

6.   What personal resources would you feel comfortable sharing with others?

READINGS

Whatever their weaknesses and failures, the first Christians were kingdom people, a community of the King. They continued the very works of Jesus, their Lord, in the spirit of Isaiah 61. They cared not only for their own, but for thousands of the poor around them. And they did so, like the Jerusalem Christians in Acts 2–5, out of the overflow of life together in Christian community. About A.D. 125 the Christian philosopher Aristides wrote,

> They walk in all humility and kindness, and falsehood is not found among them. They love one another. They despise not the widow, and grieve not the orphan. Whoever has distributes liberally to whoever has not. If they see a stranger, they bring him under their roof, and rejoice over him as if he were their own brother: for they call themselves brothers, not after the flesh, but after the Spirit of God. When one of their poor passes away from the world, and any of them see him, then he provides for his burial according to his ability; and if they hear that any of their number is imprisoned or oppressed for the name of their Messiah, all of them provide for his needs, and if it is possible that he may be delivered, they deliver him. And if there is among them a man that is poor and needy, and they have not an abundance of necessities, they fast two or three days that they may supply the needy with their necessary food.

A Kingdom Manifesto, Howard A. Snyder, InterVarsity Press, page 80.

● ● ●

In the first community, Jesus and the Twelve modeled the values of the new future of God in every dimension of life. All their relationships, including their economic ones, were transformed by the inbreaking of God's future into their midst. They shared a common purse not only among themselves, but with their followers and the poor.

The early church continued to follow the model of economic sharing Jesus had inaugurated with his community. In fact, it was a widespread practice among the early church. "Now the company of those who believed were of one heart and soul, and no one said that any of the things which he possessed was his own, but they had everything in common" (Acts 4:32, RSV).

The reason believers were able to share in this extraordinary way was that their values had been profoundly changed by Christ; they no longer lived for themselves. Their lives were devoted to the service of God, his kingdom, and his world. Through their sharing, they not only modeled the new age of economic justice; they also freed up resources for the work of justice in their own day.

As the church in the late twentieth century is renewed through a rediscovery of community, it has the opportunity to become what it was meant to be: the servant church to the world. From prison we hear Dietrich Bonhoeffer echo the cry for a servant church: "The church is only the church when it exists for others." Being the church for others means, quite simply, that we are to be a church like the one we read about in Acts—our lives, energy, and resources poured outwardly into the needy world that surrounds us.

Given the ways we use our lives, energy, and resources, are we the church for others or the church for ourselves? You will have to answer for your church. But one thing seems eminently clear to me: the church in the United States is amazingly affluent. It is reliably estimated that the total institutional wealth of all churches and religious organizations in the United States is $134.3 billion. $21 billion flows through American Christian organizations annually. "If there is anything about the Christian Church that is clear to religious and non-religious alike," asserts Adam Finnerty, "it is that some nineteen hundred...years after the birth of its founder it is a phenomenally wealthy institution. Trying to make it appear otherwise is a little like trying to hide an elephant in a phone booth." He goes on to point out that by becoming a propertied institution, it is inevitably exposed to the danger of becoming conformed to the world and allied to the world's center of power. Tony Campolo has described the church as a gigantic oil refinery with no loading dock because it uses all the oil it produces to keep its own machinery running.

Paul Brandt and Philip Yancey vividly describe what happens in a human body when one cell mutinies and begins drawing life away from the rest of the body, creating a grotesquely healthy tumor. The tumor uses up the resources necessary for the health of the rest of the body in its singleminded preoccupation with its own growth. Are we, the church in the United States, in danger of becoming not only a church for ourselves but also a cancerous tumor in the body of Jesus Christ International? How can we be the church for others when we are using most of our individual and corporate resources on our own growth?

In repentance, let's rediscover what it means to be the servant church for others. Let's look at alternative ways we might use the resources God has entrusted to us to more fully serve others. If we were to return to a network of small house churches on the model of the early church, we would soon discover we don't need most of the buildings we have been erecting for ourselves at incredible expense. At the very least, our churches have the opportunity to become much more imaginative in constructing and utilizing church properties so as to channel as few of our resources as possible away from projects of mission and service to those in need.

East Hill Church in Gresham, Oregon, grew to over forty-five hundred members by 1979. They wanted to construct a building in which the entire congregation could worship together without drawing their members' giving away from the support of their extensive programs of ministry. Their solution? They established a separate corporation to build a self-supporting convention center, which the church uses free.

In some cities, brothers and sisters from different denominations are discovering they can share a common facility.

(Some of the most underutilized structures in the United States are church buildings.) I would even go so far as to suggest a moratorium on construction of new facilities until (1) space in existing church structures, community buildings, and homes is fully utilized, (2) assessment of alternate methods of financing new structures (like the East Hill project) is made, and (3) the stewardship of our capital improvement resources in relation to the needs of the Body of Christ International is evaluated.

The Mustard Seed Conspiracy, Tom Sine, Word, pages 175–176.

● ● ●

Many of us try to find private solutions to the problem of scarce resources. We attempt to beat inflation by sending more members of the family to work. We try to stem the rising rate of crime by fortifying our homes with locks and weapons. We try to guard against catastrophic costs of serious illness by demanding more fringe benefits from our employers. We may even hoard food staples or fuel against the day when they will be unavailable in the open market.

But, as we have seen before, private solutions tend to exacerbate public problems. Hoarding diminishes the general supply; private health insurance allows medical costs to keep rising; the fortress approach to crime further isolates individuals from the public connectedness which could curb crime; growth in private purchasing power among those who already have enough only stimulates the inflationary cycle. Private solutions to the problem of scarce resources only make the resources scarcer. The greater the scarcity, the more tense becomes the public scene. And the more tense the public, the more difficult it becomes for people to look together for public solutions.

I do not think we can exaggerate the extent to which affluent Americans are caught in this vicious circle. It is said that if the earth were a global village of one hundred people, six of them would be Americans, and those six would have over one-third of the village's income. In such a village everyone would be aware of this fact; what impact would that aware-ness have on peoples' behavior? The ninety-four people who had to subsist on two-thirds of the income would surely be furious at the remaining six. And the six would surely be afraid of having their possessions, if not their lives, taken from them. The six would be unlikely to participate fully and freely in the public life. Instead, they would arm themselves, hide away as best they could, and develop elaborate rational-izations or avoidance mechanisms to deal with their "Good fortune." And that is exactly what well-to-do Americans have done, not only in relation to the Third World but also with their neighbors in poverty here at home.

The Company of Strangers, Parker J. Palmer, Crossroad, pages 93–94.

● ● ●

Background. Your car's stuck in traffic. You're late for work again. And on top of everything else, the price of gas has gone up. Why are you doing this to yourself? You could start a ridesharing project at your company. All it takes is a map, a bulletin board, and a few push-pins.

DID YOU KNOW
● Most cars on the road carry only one person. In fact, we have so much extra room in our 140 million cars that every-one in Western Europe could ride in them with us.
● It has been reported that 50% of the smog in most metro-politan areas is caused by automobile emissions.
● Commuters spent 2 billion hours stuck in traffic jams last year—and wasted about 3 billion gallons of gas in the pro-cess. That's been estimated at about 5% of our entire annual gasoline use.

WHAT YOU CAN DO
● Match up people in your company who live near each other, so they can rideshare. Here's how:
● Put up a large map of the surrounding area on a bulletin board. Give each employee a push-pin. Ask each to write his

or her name and phone number on a small piece of paper, and pin it on the map to show where each of them lives.

● List people who live near each other, and distribute the list to your co-workers.

● Ask your employer to provide incentives to encourage ridesharing. One idea: Give carpoolers free parking spaces, and charge solo commuters a fee to park.

_____

The Next Step: 50 More Things You Can Do to Save the Earth, The Earthworks Group, Andrews and McMeel, page 63.

● ● ●

For example, our sharing at the meeting revealed that several agencies gave away clothing. The duplication was actually convenient for the agencies. In Holland [Michigan] there was no shortage of donated clothing, and so there was no reason to ration its distribution. Imposing more accountability on the distribution of clothing would reduce distribution and thereby produce a stockpile of clothing. This would require renting a warehouse. In addition, controlling distribution at each agency and coordinating distribution among the agencies would take a lot of time. The agencies saved money and time by simply giving away clothing to anyone who asked. But, one agency representative pointed out, it was apparent that some people were showing up at one agency after another asking for clothes. It turned out that some of these people simply never did laundry. When clothes got dirty, they threw them away and went back for more. After all, if you don't have your own washing machine, why go through the bother of going to a laundromat, as long as clean clothes are always available?

Who was responsible for this behavior? Surely the agencies contributed to it by their own irresponsible style of compassion.

The same was true of financial aid. Whenever assistance is readily available, people will take advantage of it and may not even think they are acting irresponsibly. Why should a person feel guilty about accepting something that an agency or church readily provides? (An especially memorable instance of financial irresponsibility was a client's request that a church donate money to pay his fine for welfare fraud!)

It was incredibly frustrating to realize that our way of doing things unintentionally kept people focused exclusively on their physical needs. We made it virtually impossible for them to achieve any level of self-esteem, because the helping experience was not designed to give them the help they really needed to become self-sufficient; it was geared to meeting their needs for clothing, money or whatever, in the manner that was simplest for us. Much of the blame for chronic dependence lay with the service providers, who lacked the resources and relationships with other providers to intervene more deeply in their lives. The system was betraying people.

The agency representatives reached the decision to work together more closely. In a series of meetings in the fall of 1976 we systematically gathered information about needs and resources in the Holland area. We conceived of a clearinghouse that would interview people to determine their needs and would refer them to the appropriate agencies for help. We developed a policy statement for the clearinghouse and even came up with a name—Love, Inc.

We agreed that the clearinghouse:

● should not promote any further duplication of efforts in town;

● should conduct a need analysis of each client to determine the nature, extent and legitimacy of his or her needs;

● should identify people who were chronically dependent, not with the intention of dismissing their needs but in order to understand their whole need and to involve them in the process of overcoming their irresponsible behavior;

● should confirm the availability of help at an agency before referring someone to it.

Helping agencies would work cooperatively in analyzing people's expressed needs. The clearinghouse would become a city-wide data bank on people having a wide variety of needs.

The next question was how to use the clearinghouse to bring these needy people into direct contact with church members. I suggested to the agency people that the clearinghouse could be used to connect needy people not only with appropriate agencies but also with church members who could help them. Doing this, I argued, would be a way of enlisting more people, more resources, in helping needy people in the community.

The agency staff members were not optimistic about this proposal. Their general view was that the churches were irrelevant to meeting needs. Staff members cited instances in which churches had unnecessarily duplicated services or had started out to provide help but then lost interest. Agencies expressed their sense of responsibility to protect their clients from church members' passing enthusiasms. They were interested in asking churches for food, clothing and money, and even for volunteers for programs. They did not, however, envision making the churches partners with them in helping the needy members of the community.

One reason agencies did not perceive a need for church members was that the war on poverty had produced a multitude of organizations and funding streams. Agencies had appeared to meet every need. The proliferation of well-funded agencies for a while masked the fact that agency efforts unfortunately often did not alleviate the needs or eliminate poverty. The spending cuts of the 1980s would force agencies to cast about for new resources. The possibility that church members might be enlisted became more attractive as it became clear that they represented not a reshuffling of existing resources but an infusion of new ones.

In any case, in 1976, despite reservations, the agency workers admitted that a cooperative program with church members would be great if it worked.

The next step, then, was for me to go to the churches.

Help Is Just around the Corner, Virgil Gulker with Kevin Perrotta, Creation House, pages 50–53.

CHAPTER FOUR
RELATING EMPATHETICALLY

In a setting characterized by a lot of changes, it's hard for people to be understanding and tolerant. The more typical response is to stake out their turf and furiously defend it.

For example, a new worker is not always welcomed with open arms by fellow employees. They're nervous about how this newcomer will affect their roles. All kinds of jockeying for position ensues.

A similar sense of discomfort can surface in a family as it grows. A new baby may mean a change in relationships, which sometimes results in unexpected hostility on the part of another child.

In the bigger setting, shifts in a society often lead to polarization. When there's uncertainty about what's going to happen, people become defensive of their position and intolerant of any who threaten it. We see this presently throughout the former Soviet Union. As the Commonwealth of Independent States attempts to stabilize, territorial wars have broken out in a number of areas.

Let me give an illustration from our own history. We had Indian wars in America from the time of the first European settlements until the massacre of the Sioux in 1890 at Wounded Knee Creek in South Dakota. The shift in the color of America's skin from red to white hardly occurred as a result of fair negotiations. But for a long time in our history books, it was easier to explain what happened from the biased white perspective. That meant picturing native Americans as the ones doing all the attacking, infringing on the rights of whites, and being little more than savages.

It's taken a hundred years for us to reexamine that strongly held position. Now we admit—somewhat reluctantly—that in the three centuries of fighting that went on, whites were not always the "good guys."

Dances With Wolves starring Kevin Costner, told the soldiers' and Indians' story in a new way. This time the Native Americans were portrayed as being more humane than the men in military uniforms.

The book jacket of this number one best-seller by Michael Blake reads: "When a drunken major ordered Lieutenant John Dunbar to an abandoned army post, the war-weary soldier suddenly found himself alone, beyond the edge of civilization, with only a wolf and some roving Commanches for company.

"Thievery and survival soon forced Dunbar into the Indian camp, where he began a dangerous adventure that changed his life forever. Each day in the wilderness, Dunbar became more Indian, learning the ways of a proud and glorious people. But when his past came back to haunt him and he was faced with the greatest decision of his life, Dunbar discovered who the real savages were and where his loyalty lay...."

One of the Indian warriors, Wind In His Hair, was a somewhat impulsive man. In time he would save Dunbar's life. But the struggle these two had, first just to understand one another, and then to become friends, is a miniature picture of the national dilemma at that time. Basic personalities of these two men were different, they didn't speak the same language, and their customers were bewildering to each other. But both men worked at the relationship.

At the end of the film there is a powerful scene. Sought by the military as a deserter, Dunbar and his wife have to leave the camp. The army is closing in on his location. It is a bitter cold day, and snow is falling. The white man and his wife gather their belongings, say their sad good-byes, and are on their way, when from a hill high above them, they hear a shout. It's an Indian sitting on his pony. In his right hand he holds a lance above his head as he yells, "Dances With Wolves, I am Wind In His Hair. Do you see that I am your friend? Can you see that you will always be my friend?" And in spite of all the pain-filled events surrounding this scene, these two men give us hope and show that reconciliation can take place if people will only work at it.

I'm reminded of the story of a Methodist circuit-riding preacher who visited an Indian village. As he sat by the campfire with members of the tribe, he tried to come up with a way to witness for Christ. Finally he said, "I have been thinking about a rule given by the Son of the God I worship. People have thought it so wonderful, they've called it the Golden Rule."

"Don't praise it," responded the chief, "tell me what it is, and I'll decide whether or not it's golden."

So the frontier preacher continued, "It was Jesus, who came here from heaven, who said, 'Do unto others, as you would have them do unto you.' In other words, the way you want people to treat you is the way you should treat them."

"Ah," said the chief, dismissing the thought, "It cannot be done!" Then there was silence while the minister tried to think of another approach. But he didn't have to, because after pondering the matter further the chief remarked, "I have been considering what you said. If the Great Spirit who made man would also give him a new heart, then He could do as you say. But only then."

How wonderful that this is exactly what God has done for those who are His. He's given us a new heart, so now we can treat others the way we ourselves want to be treated. It's not necessary to argue and fight and kill, always living fearfully and defensively and in hostility. We can be agents of reconciliation because of the new heart given us by our Great Holy Spirit.

Polarization

This is a day of increasing polarization. Instead of coming together, the various segments of our society are pulling apart. *Polarization* comes from the word *polarity*, which relates to opposite magnetic fields. When you try to bring these fields together, they move apart instead. More and more that's the way elements of North American society are reacting to one another:

—Male and female

—Young and old
—Pro-Life and Pro-Choice
—Black and white
—Privileged and powerless

They've been more used to warring than to working together. Like Jew and Arab, they no longer trust one another. Reconciliation means to bring together warring parties. It's one of God's specialities. And in this day reconciliation needs to mark the people of God to a much greater extent. Differences will remain, and powerful forces of the old way will continue to try to destroy us. But ours is the defiant cry from the ledge above: "Dances With Wolves, I am Wind In His Hair. Do you see that I am your friend? Can you see that you will always be my friend?"

Relating empathetically is a survival skill desperately needed in the world today. Gathering armies to see which side is strongest has been tried time and again. That tactic may resolve some problems, but the cost to everyone is immense.

Relating empathetically says:

I'm not going to just shout my thoughts at you. First, I'm going to listen to what you're saying. I'm going to try to understand where you're coming from. When I'm confused about your viewpoint, I'm going to ask questions. If I don't agree with you, at least I'll comprehend why you feel the way you do. But most of all, I want you to know that I value you as a person, even if our positions are incompatible. And I'm treating you this way because in the most important relationship in my life, this is how I have been treated.

You see, as Paul writes in Colossians 1, I once was alienated from God, an enemy in my mind, characterized by evil behavior. But instead of overpowering me by His superior force, God overwhelmed me with His love. Through His Son Jesus Christ, He changed me and made me holy in His sight, without blemish, free from accusation. If God can relate that way to me in spite of our immense differences, I believe I can respond that way to others when we differ on a much smaller scale.

Have you ever been in a situation where you felt like the odd man out (or odd woman out)? Maybe you remember driving all alone afterward, nursing your wounds and thinking, "If only ... if only I knew where I could go to sit in a large group and hear a lecture. That would be so wonderful right now!"

If you've never had that experience, it's because what you wanted was a sympathetic friend, not a lecture. You needed someone to whom you could vent your feelings and share your hurt. You certainly weren't looking for a person who would quickly respond, "I believe I understand; now let me tell you what you need to do to get out of this stupid mood." When you feel alienated, what you need is a listening ear.

I don't know why the church doesn't understand that. We put so much emphasis on preaching, and that's important. But it's hardly the most appealing way to approach people in a polarized society — getting them to come and sit in a large group and listen to a lecture.

Let me take this a step further. Because lecture is the communication technique the church models most, it's little wonder that even outside our sanctuaries Christians most often approach others by TELLING THEM what the truth is they need to hear.

It's almost as if we've lost the ability to befriend people who aren't exactly like us, to get to know them and discover why they think and act the way they do. It seems it would be more effective to share our beliefs in a more natural fashion after we've first laid the appropriate groundwork.

But this approach is very uncomfortable for the great majority of Christians today. It requires that we truly care about the other person, even if she's pro-choice in her view on abortion, for example. Or, it's saying to a businessman, "I know we may disagree on how your housing development will affect the environment in this area, but that doesn't mean I should despise you as a person. Now tell me again where you're coming from. Then let me repeat what I hear you saying, to see if I'm understanding you accurately."

Relating empathetically is learning the skill Jesus had developed so well, of hating sin but caring deeply for the sinner.

Isn't that what the Incarnation was all about? God got into our skin for the sake of identifying with us. Amazing, isn't it? He doesn't just shout His truth from heaven, saying, "Here's how it is, you turkeys, take it or else!"

Hebrews 4:15 tells us that Christ is able to sympathize with our weaknesses, because He was tempted in every way as we are—including feeling rejected. Jesus remembers what it was like to be hated by powerful people who wanted to have Him killed, and who got their way. How's that for a crash course on the results of polarization?

And I know that Christ often preached to the multitudes, but He also let people ask Him questions. He had a running debate going with the religious authorities. Debate is a two-way communication.

Then Jesus was always asking questions of His own:
- "Who do people say I am?" (Mark 8:27)
- "John's baptism—was it from heaven, or from men?" (11:30)
- "If I drive out demons by Beelzebub, by whom do your people drive them out?" (Matt. 12:27)
- "What shall we say the kingdom of God is like?" (Mark 4:30)
- "Who appointed Me a judge or an arbiter between you?" (Luke 12:14)
- "What are you discussing together?" (24:17)

Christ would do well in our society. His communication skills were so diverse. I can't picture Him saying, "I won't be on 'The Tonight Show' unless you let Me preach a sermon." I bet He would say yes to the invitation and then show great respect for the host as a person. Rather than giving a sermon, I suspect that Jesus would take the opportunity to tell a pointed story or two. Maybe He'd offer the one about the son who wasted his inheritance and ended up eating with the pigs until he came to his senses and returned home.

Variety of Communication Forms

To survive and be strong, I believe, the church must learn to imitate Christ's ways of relating to others. Church leaders need to encourage a variety of communication forms, rather than focusing exclusively on preaching.

We assume that in New Testament times, believers went to church services much the same as ours. But that's not true. There was far more exchange between worshipers than we experience now. For the most part, the early Christians met in homes. That's a more inviting place to take a friend than to a lecture hall.

As modern Christians, if we want to survive our times and be anything more than an isolated subculture, we need to reach out in ways other than, "I'm sorry, this is God's truth, so take it or else!"

Proverbs 18:13 reads, "He who answers before listening— that is his folly and his shame."

The skill of relating sensitively—of listening and trying to understand what the other person is feeling, of allowing time for a friendship to develop—this is what will bring together the opposing segments of our culture. In short, the ability to relate empathetically can counter the trend toward polarization in our shifting society.

I learned that lesson during the decade I worked in the inner city of Chicago. Fortunately, there were some wise people in my congregation who advised me, "Don't come into this neighborhood and tell people what they need, as though they didn't have enough sense to figure out where they're hurting. Ask them! Meet those needs as you can, and in time you'll earn the right to talk with them about Christ." That was good counsel.

Even within the church we must become much more adept at asking questions. We need to find out, after a three-month study of Romans, for example, if people really understand what the epistle is all about. Are they growing in the Lord? Have they gotten to know one another better during these weeks?

Children of a Lesser God is a powerful play. It has two leading characters. One is James Leeds, who is thirtyish and a speech teacher at a State School for the Deaf. Sarah Norman is in her mid-twenties. She has been deaf from birth.

When James talks to Sarah, he signs because she can't read lips. So that the audience can understand, he speaks over what he says with his hands.

When Sarah signs in response, James tells us what she is saying. It's amazing how interesting the play is, and how beautiful her hand movements are. It's a rare treat to "watch" her talk. By the end of Act One, these two have fallen in love and are married.

Reading from the jacket of the book: "What sets this action apart is the circumstance of Sarah's total deafness. And her refusal to voice words. At 26, although of college calibre, she works as a maid in the school for the deaf where James has become a teacher. Here she hides in silence her scars of early rejection and fears of being thought retarded because of the odd sounds she would make.

"With great good humor and intelligence, James, hiding his own psychic wounds, faces the difficulties of his marriage and his determination to bring Sarah, who only 'signs' into the hearing world."

I saw this play some years ago, but I still remember the pressure James puts on Sarah all through the play. He's insistent that he knows what's best for her. As the tension peaks, he says in exasperation: "You can cook, but you can't speak. . . . You always have to be dependent on someone, and you always will for the rest of your life until you learn to speak. Now come on! I want you to speak to me. Let me hear it. Speak! Speak! Speak!"

Finally Sarah succumbs and an awful sound erupts. It hardly seems like words, only passion. We barely pick up snatches of phrases like, "How do you like my voice? . . . Am I what you want me to be? What about me? What I want?"

Shocked at how badly Sarah speaks, James reaches to touch her, but she bolts away.

Too often we are like James Leeds. We make our demands. We say, in effect, "This is what you have to do — right now — and my way." And we have no idea how deeply the other person may be feeling wounded or shamed. We just want done what we want done — and NOW!

Lord Jesus,
I praise You that when You walked this earth You minis-

tered to people where they hurt. You were sensitive to
the deaf, the blind, the leprous, the demon-possessed.
Help us to offer your healing touch to others, in ways
that go beyond mere words. Teach us to relate empathetically.
Amen.

FOR DISCUSSION AND REFLECTION

1.   Do you agree that our society is becoming increas-
      ingly polarized? Give reasons for your answer.

2.   How good are you at relating empathetically with
      people whose views on basic issues differ from your
      own?

3.   What kind of person is hardest for you to get along
      with?

4.   How skilled are you at asking people perceptive
      questions?

5.   "Survival skill" is a strong term. Is it an overstate-
      ment to call relating empathetically a survival skill?
      Why or why not?

6.   The church seems to focus on lecture as its primary means of communication. What other communication tools do you think the church should develop?

READINGS

Really seeking to understand another person is probably one of the most important deposits you can make, and it is the key to every other deposit. You simply don't know what constitutes a deposit to another person until you understand that individual. What might be a deposit for you—going for a walk to talk things over, going out for ice cream together, working on a common project—might not be perceived by someone else as a deposit at all. It might even be perceived as a withdrawal, if it doesn't touch the person's deep interests or needs.

One person's mission is another person's minutia. To make a deposit, what is important to another person must be as important to you as the other person is to you. You may be working on a high priority project when your six-year-old child interrupts with something that seems trivial to you, but it may be very important from his point of view. . . . By accepting the value he places on what he has to say, you show an understanding of him that makes a great deposit.

I have a friend whose son developed and avid interest in baseball. My friend wasn't interested in baseball at all. But one summer, he took his son to see every major league team play one game. The trip took over six weeks and cost a great deal of money, but it became a powerful bonding experience in their relationship.

My friend was asked on his return, "Do you like baseball that much?"

"No," he replied, "but I like my son that much."

The Seven Habits of Highly Effective People, Stephen R. Covey, Fireside/Simon & Schuster, pages 190–191.

● ● ●

In my earlier work I emphasized that women may get the impression men aren't listening to them even when the men really are. *This happens because men have different habitual ways of showing they're listening. As anthropologists Maltz and Borker explain, women are more inclined to ask questions. They also give more listening response—little words like mhm, uh-uh, and yeah—sprinkled throughout someone else's talk, providing a running feedback loop. And they respond more positively and enthusiastically, for example by agreeing and laughing.*

All this behavior is doing the work of listening. It also creates rapport-talk by emphasizing connection and encouraging more talk. The corresponding strategies of men—giving fewer listener responses, making statements rather than asking questions, and challenging rather than agreeing—can be understood as moves in a contest by incipient speakers rather than audience members.

Not only do women give more listening signals, according to Maltz and Borker, but the signals they give have different meanings for men and women, consistent with the speaker/audience alignment. Women use "yeah" to mean "I'm with you, I follow," whereas men tend to say "yeah" only when they agree. The opportunity for misunderstanding is clear. When a man is confronted with a woman who has been saying "yeah," "yeah," "yeah," and then turns out not to agree, he may conclude that she has been insincere, or that she was agreeing without really listening. When a woman is confronted with a man who does *not* say "yeah,"—or much of anything else—she may conclude that *he* hasn't been listening. *The men's style is more literally focused on the message level of talk, while the women's is focused on the relationship or metamessage level.*

To a man who expects a listener to be quietly attentive, a woman giving a stream of feedback and support will seem to be talking too much for a listener. To a woman who expects a listener to be active and enthusiastic in showing interest, attention, and support, a man who listens silently will seem not to be listening at all, but rather to have checked out of the conversation, taken his listening marbles, and gone mentally home.

Because of these patterns, women may get the impression that men aren't listening when they really are. But I have come to understand, more recently, that it is also true that men listen to women less frequently than women listen to men, because the act of listening has different meanings for them. Some men really *don't* want to listen at length because they feel it frames them as subordinate. Many women do want to listen, but they expect it to be reciprocal—I listen to you now; you listen to me later. They become frustrated when they do the listening now and now and now, and later never comes.

You Just Don't Understand, Deborah Tannen, William Morrow and Company, pages 142–143.

● ● ●

Empathy is that process in which you imaginatively put yourself in the place of the other person. Interpathy recognizes that you cannot do this, but you are eager to learn from the other person what his or her being is like. If you and I have not come from a heritage of personal humiliation, derogation, and ridicule, we are a little phony when we say that we "know" what it is like. Yet we share a common passion for justice and want them to teach us about the injustices they have suffered. If we have not been premature, there is hope that a genuine alliance can thus be formed and sustained. If we too quickly convey that we "know" just how they feel, they can more quickly tell us, "Nobody knows the trouble I've seen."

Behind the Masks, Wayne E. Oates, The Westminster Press, pages 105–106.

● ● ●

It may seem strange to begin our overview of verbal communication contrasts with *listening* instead of *talking*. But remember, this is aimed at *parents*. And as painful as it may be to admit, some of us fail to really listen to our children. Sometimes this includes me, I regret to say.

When Dave was in high school, he once asked me to stop

mixing cookie dough and listen to him. I said that I *had* been listening, to which he replied, "I don't feel like you hear me when you won't stop and look at me."

Zap! I felt as if I'd taken a bullet in the heart. I suddenly realized that I'd been doing that to Dave and Becky for years. Sure, I had read about how parents could improve communication with children: I knew the importance of eye contact to make the other person feel "heard." What I did *not* know was how much my childhood learning short-circuited good communication principles.

I grew up believing that doing only one thing at a time was inexcusably inefficient. I specialized in multiplying my daily allotment of moments by cramming most of them with at least two activities. I was feeling smugly satisfied with myself, actually, on the afternoon of Dave's request: I was baking cookies and listening to him at the same time. But that afternoon, Dave needed a "laying on of ears and eyes" more than a plateful of warm cookies.

Reflecting on that experience, I see that throughout much of my parenting, I focused more on *doing for* than on *being with* my children. Many times this shame-based preoccupation with productivity interfered with respectfully listening to Dave and Becky with my undivided attention.

Perhaps our greatest obstacle to listening is our own desire to talk. Often we're like the man invited to give a brief talk at his Yale alumni meeting. Using the four letters in Yale as an outline, he waxed eloquent and long on each: *Y*outh, *A*chievement, *L*oyalty and finally *E*nthusiasm. When he finished his "brief" talk nearly two hours later, a bored guest whispered to a companion, "I'm sure glad he didn't graduate from the Massachusetts Institute of Technology!"

As parents, our "talks" frequently become lengthy lectures or sermons. This is easy to understand when we consider that many of us grew up with parents who were "talk terrorists." While lobbing verbal hand grenades and detonating deadly word-bombs (often *very* sweetly), they taught us that parents possess the inalienable right to talk without listening. They made it as clear to us as their parents had to them: "Children are to be seen and not heard."

Now that *we* are the parents, we want to stamp our feet and shout, *"My* turn, *my* turn!"* However, our children have this annoying habit of wanting us to listen—*really listen*—to them. (Remember back when you still indulged that desire, before you surrendered it to inescapable barrages of parental verbiage—or perhaps to stone-silent stares?) This is a significant choice point for those of us longing to become shame-free parents. Will we "take our turn" and continue the family pattern? Or will we begin listening to understand with eyes and ears?

Here's something to consider when weighing this choice. First, some of us have begun to suspect that we don't understand our children much better than our folks understood us. Second, we learn more about our children by listening to them than by talking at them. If this is true, then we may "discover" our children more fully than ever before when we "pay the price" to become better listeners. The cost of this priceless discovery? We must willingly relinquish our turn at terrorist talking.

Another reason we need to listen to our children is to help them learn problem-solving skills. This may be one hundred eighty degrees from our own childhood experiences. In most dysfunctional families, when a child takes a problem to parents they tend to ignore it or "solve" it themselves by imposing their own ideas.

What a contrast to healthier families where parents respond by asking something like, "What ideas have you thought of?" Parents then help their children generate and evaluate various solution options and potential outcomes. This process takes some time and it requires that both the parents and the children listen, think and talk.

Shame-Free Parenting, Sandra Wilson, InterVarsity Press, pages 123–125.

● ● ●

Have you ever gone to church, talked with a number of people, but returned home with the strange feeling that you were all alone or uncared for? Maybe you spoke to a dozen individuals, yet you shared nothing of real substance with any of them. You didn't get to know anyone better, and no one made an effort to get close to you.

"How are you?" "You sure look good in that outfit." "Nice day, isn't it?" "Work going well?" "Great to see you again." Talk can be superficial. Though it seems friendly, when all is said and done, there's not much to latch on to. Some people in the congregation might know your name, where you work, or how many kids you have. But few discover the inner you.

Why do so many of us have difficulty getting past surface talk? Most of us long for deeper relationships. But even if we were to spend an entire evening with a group from the church, we still might come away knowing very little about the other people who were there.

What do people talk about? Sports, movies, television, school, recipes, personalities, books, the weather ... the list goes on. But that's hardly what's important to us.

So, what seems to be the problem? Part of the difficulty has to do with conversational skills. More specifically, most church people aren't adept at asking good questions.

Case in point: you're in church and the minister says, "Would visitors please raise your hands?" In a healthy congregation, that might involve ten or fifteen people. Then the pastor announces, "We'd like to take a few minutes to get to know one another. Would those of you who are regulars please greet our visitors and make them feel at home?"

But too often the conversation goes nowhere. "You're a visitor?" "Yes." "First time here, huh?" "That's right." "Never been to this church before?" "No." "Good to have you!" "Thank you." Sound too familiar? Such exchanges take place time and time again. We just aren't able to get beyond the old standbys.

Obviously, "Are you a visitor?" could be improved on. Why? Because the person is limited in terms of how he or she can answer. Most likely the response will be, "Yes, I am." That's like asking, "How are you?" Most people will say, "Fine, thanks." Then the exchange dies and another opportunity to get to know someone is gone.

It's much better to work at asking questions that allow the

other person to reveal something more significant. For example, if you ask, "Where do you work?" most likely you'll get a quick answer. The conversation won't go anywhere. But, if you add, " ... and what's something you enjoy about your job?" you open a window that can reveal more about that person.

Granted, it's hard to ask a meaningful question when you only have about thirty seconds to talk to somebody. But everyone should be able to come up with a good question to ask a visitor after the service is dismissed. Rarely does this ever happen, however. Week after week, year after year, some people say the same things over and over. Would you believe it's common to find longtime members in our churches who still feel like nobody really knows them? Sad, isn't it?

Getting Beyond "How Are You?" David Mains and Melissa Timberlake, Victor Books, pages 5–7.

CHAPTER FIVE

GUARDING SELF-RESPECT

Your world is wobbling. You've lost your job and can't find another one. Or, your spouse has filed for divorce. The doctor says you have a tumor that could be malignant. Maybe it's just that you're getting quite a bit older and you wish you could turn back the clock. Whatever it is, the situation has shaken you.

I Am God's Child

I recall driving down to the south side of Chicago over twenty years ago for Operation Push rallies. Jesse Jackson would preach every week to large crowds of blacks, many of them poor. To them Jesse represented hope. Often he would get the people to chant with him. "I may be poor," he would lead out, and they would respond, *I may be poor.* "I may be on welfare," he would continue, and they would repeat, *I may be on welfare.* "I may not have a job." *I may not have a job.* "But I am..." *But I am...* "Somebody..." *Somebody...* "I am..." *I am...* "God's child." *God's child.* Then everyone would clap because the truth was powerful and freeing. And it needed to be rehearsed over and over because too often the world shouted at these people, "You are nothing!"

In these changing times, many individuals—not just African Americans—need to be convinced of this truth. "I am somebody. I am God's child."

"Know," writes the psalmist, "that the Lord is God. It is He who made us, and we are His" (Ps. 100:3). That truth seems so basic, you might think it hardly worth mentioning. Yet a lot of Christians don't live in the reality of the psalmist's words.

Actually, that's the first truth taught in the Scriptures. It's the doctrine of Creation. Men and women are not the products of mere time and chance. Rather, it's God Himself who made us. As human beings we are the pinnacle of God's handiwork. He has given us dominion over all the rest of His creation. The most complex of His creatures, human beings have great dignity in this world.

Too often in our presentation of the Gospel we start with point two, that humanity has fallen, that we've sinned. But our hearers will fail to comprehend how great a fall that was if we don't establish upfront that man and woman were first wonderful, that they were made by God with tremendous potential for good.

I'm not saying that we can earn our salvation. Our own righteousness falls hopelessly short of the payment necessary to cover the cost of our sin. But my point is that I am wonderful and you are wonderful, because we bear this stamp: "MADE BY GOD IN HIS IMAGE." In Psalm 139:14, David says, "I praise You because I am fearfully and wonderfully made; Your works are wonderful, I know that full well."

How sad that in spite of such a marvelous beginning, I sinned. Like you, I fell from this high position of privilege. But the good news is that through Christ we can be restored. Not only can we be forgiven, we can once again be filled with the Spirit of God. As the Lord breathed His spirit into Adam when He formed him from the dust, so He can make our bodies places where He Himself dwells by His Holy Spirit.

Originally we were wonderful. Yes, we fell because of sin. But, praise the Lord, we can be restored to the original design.

How foolish it would be to fight for a creationist viewpoint that had significance only in the battle against evolution. The doctrine of Creation is also vitally important because of what it does for us personally. Because of God's Creation, and the work of Christ to restore us to what was intended all along, men and women have immense worth.

Later in Genesis, where we read about the creation of Adam and Eve, we encounter another interesting character. Recently a musical was made about him called *Joseph and the*

Amazing Technicolor Dreamcoat. This is one of those situations where I'll stick with the book because it's better than the play!

It's Genesis 37, and Joseph is loved more by his father than are any of his eleven brothers. At the time Joseph is seventeen and the oldest son of Jacob's favorite wife, Rachel, who's now dead. Blessed with good looks, Joseph is honored by his father with a richly ornamented robe that soon will get him into trouble.

You know the story. His jealous older brothers attack him, strip him of this hated symbol of favoritism, and then leave him in a cistern. Though he screams to be freed, their hearts are calloused, and they sit down to eat their lunch. When a caravan of Ishmaelites comes along, an idea is hatched. "Let's sell Joseph and that way we won't have to kill him." So a purchase price is agreed on—twenty shekels of silver.

For this young man that's quite a tumble from a position of privilege, isn't it? From favorite son of a rich father, to shackled prisoner being marched into Egypt, you're on your way to be sold at the slave auction, Joseph. Better repeat after me, not out loud, but say the words to yourself: I may be a prisoner. *I may be a prisoner.* I may be naked. *I may be naked.* I may be sold as a slave—Say it! *No.* Say it: *I may be sold as a slave.* But I am . . . *But I am.* Somebody. *Somebody.* I am . . . *I am* . . . God's child. *God's child.*

Joseph is bought by a man named Potiphar, who is one of Pharaoh's officials. Before long, because of the good job Joseph does, he is put in charge of everything Potiphar owns. In Genesis 39, we read, "Now Joseph was well-built and handsome, and after a while his master's wife took notice of Joseph and said, 'Come to bed with me!' But he refused. . . . And though she spoke to Joseph day after day, he refused to go to bed with her or even be with her" (vv. 6-8, 10).

Young Joseph pays a price for being righteous. The rejected woman fabricates a story. She tells her husband that Joseph tried to take advantage of her sexually. Once again Joseph's world wobbles as he's jailed with the king's prisoners.

Down through the years, many believers have been imprisoned unfairly. It's a humiliating experience, to say the least.

Do you suppose some of them have repeated:
I may be in jail. *I may be in jail.*
I may be treated unfairly. *I may be treated unfairly.*
But I am still . . . *But I am still . . .*
Somebody. *Somebody.*
I bear the mark
MADE BY GOD.
And though broken because of sin,
I've been restored by Christ.
Hallelujah! *Hallelujah!*

In time, Joseph is released from prison and made the number-two leader in all the land of Egypt. Everyone knows his name and his face. A chariot races down a government street. The rider reins his horse. When the dust settles a bit, you see the license plate—"No. 2." That's Joseph. He's somebody, and everybody agrees with that assessment.

But Joseph is the same person who not long ago was in prison—and before that was standing on the auction block. He hasn't changed, only the circumstances have. In God's eyes he's always been quite special!

Have you learned the Joseph lesson? At work it doesn't matter whether someone answers to you or you now answer to that someone. Those kinds of things shift a lot. Maybe you've been laid off because, with new technology, your best skills aren't needed anymore. Or maybe you're a professional musician whose style was popular for a season but not anymore.

You Are Somebody
Know this: You are still somebody. You are the marvelous product of an infinite God's creative genius, and He doesn't make cheap stuff. Yes, a sin defect showed up in you as in everyone else. But the Lord went to great pains to correct that problem as well. Why? Because you're someone special.

The world may say you're just another nameless nobody.
You're not handsome.
You're not beautiful.
You're not brilliant.
You're not highly talented.

You're not wealthy.

You're not famous or powerful.

Maybe you've been lead to believe you're second class because:

You're not employed.

Or you're not married.

Or you're not white.

Or you're not male.

Or you're not a graduate.

Or you're not an adult yet.

Or, for one reason or another, you're not worth paying attention to!

To survive those kinds of messages, you need to keep telling yourself the truth.

I am somebody.

I am not a product of mere time and chance.

I am God's child, by birth and by rebirth.

I have great value.

I should not sell myself short.

I must guard my self-respect.

I won't always be in this tough spot.

The Lord is working in my behalf—I know He is.

I am a favorite of my wealthy Father.

In fact, I have a robe, a technicolor dreamcoat He's holding for me.

And I will live this day with that truth fixed in my mind.

I would be a fool to do otherwise.

"Know this . . ." writes the psalmist, and I repeat his words. "Know that the Lord is God. It is He who made us, and we are His." Reciting words of affirmation, as Jesse Jackson taught, was a survival skill for many poor blacks in the 1960s. Today, this skill can prove a valuable help for another wide swath of God's people, as they say to themselves, *Know this: I am somebody! I am God's child.*

When we don't continually remind ourselves that our worth comes from God, we tend to look to others for affirmation. And if they don't say what we want to hear, we attempt to resolve the problem on our own:

—We say in self-pity, "I'm not appreciated at this place the way I should be."

—Or we boast, "You should have seen the changes in the way that committee functioned once I became chairperson. I tell you, it was awesome!"

—Or we fish for a compliment: "Did you like the table decorations at the Sunday School banquet?"

Rubbish. Do you know what rubbish is? It's not the garbage, the food waste. Rubbish is the trash, the household things we throw away because they're worthless.

Well, that's what you can do with the affirmation needs you have, once you truly understand who you are in God and in Christ. You can take those desires for approval from others and toss them in the trash.

The truth is, the ultimate compliment is to have the God of the universe say, "You have great value." And the supreme irony is that, for whatever reason, many of us are not able to hear His words of affirmation.

Are we special because of what we've done? Of course not. Our worth is based on God's opinion of us and, more specifically, on what He's done in our behalf through Christ. We "glory in Christ," writes Paul in Philippians 3, and "put no confidence in the flesh." The apostle continues: "If anyone else thinks he has reasons to put confidence in the flesh, I have more." And then he reluctantly lists his credentials. But of those accomplishments Paul comments, "I consider them rubbish, that I may gain Christ" (vv. 3-4, 8).

In other words, Paul is saying, "That list of what I've done, spiritually speaking, is trash to be tossed out and never again sorted through. Let the waste company figure out what to do with it. I'm paying them to pick it up as junk. Rubbish! Because here's who I am (and I am somebody): I am God's child! Nothing can top that!"

We might say something similar.

—If I am affirmed by the media as talented, successful, important, but God is nowhere to be found in my life, is that a good position to be in?

—If I have a wonderful, high-paying job, but a terrible relationship with the Lord, what good is that?

—If friends fill my life, but when I'm alone I have no one to turn to who will hear me pray, what have I gained?

Our Source of Identity

Just as Paul says, our primary source of identity must be Christ, and then we'll be all right whether we're struggling or riding the crest. Whether, like Joseph, we're in prison or holding a position of prominence, whether our world is wobbling or rotating so smoothly it hums. Either way, we know who we are. Nothing can take that from us.

Believe me, I know this is a hard-won victory. It doesn't come easily. There aren't many in the church who truly understand Paul's words about self-worth. Frequently in Christian circles, the subject isn't addressed at all.

So when hard times come, we have to help one another. When the world begins to wobble on us, it's important to help others guard their self-respect, to remind them that none of us are mere victims of the capricious winds of change. God is still in His heaven. Our Maker knows what is happening to His children. He cares, He truly does. And through Christ, He has fashioned a whole new family where there's great strength if we support one another. The "every man for himself" mind-set does not belong in the church.

From the very beginning of His ministry, Jesus encouraged His followers not to be judgmental, but supportive. He knew it would be tough enough just to be one of His disciples in that day. So he asked them, "Why do you look at the speck of sawdust in your brother's eye and pay no attention to the plank in your own eye? How can you say to your brother, 'Let me take the speck out of your eye,' when all the time there is a plank in your own eye?" (Matt. 7:3-4)

Great humor, isn't it? But Jesus still makes His point. Don't always be looking for the other guy's flaw. Instead, guard one another's self-respect, especially if you want to survive times like these.

Is that what you do? I hope so, for Jesus' sake—and for the sake of others and your own sake as well.

Driving Miss Daisy, by Alfred Uhry, is a play that won the 1988 Pulitzer Prize. Later it was made into a film starring Jessica Tandy and Morgan Freeman. It's one of those humorous, gentle, surprising stories that slowly draws you in, allowing you gradually to get to know the two main characters.

Miss Daisy is a Jewish widow living in Atlanta, who needs a chauffeur because she's gotten too old to drive. But she's spirited and crusty and prejudiced against blacks—although she insists that she's not.

Hoke Coleburn is sixty when he's hired for the job by Daisy's son, Boolie. Hoke is "colored," which is the term used for African Americans in 1948, the year the play begins. He's both simple and wise, a wonderful character, with certain stereotypical ideas about what Jews are like.

Both Hoke and Miss Daisy are unique personalities, and as a Jew and a black, each represents a race of people who have had to learn a great deal about guarding self-respect.

Daisy doesn't want her son to hire a driver, and she tells him so. "I am seventy-two years old as you so gallantly reminded me and I am a widow, but unless they rewrote the Constitution and didn't tell me, I still have my rights. And one of my rights is the right to invite who I want—not who you want—into my house. You do accept the fact that this is my house? What I do not want—and absolutely will not have is some—some chauffeur sitting in my kitchen, gobbling my food, running up my phone bill."

But as I already mentioned, Hoke is hired. The play is about his relationship with Miss Daisy, which spans twenty-five years. As they learn about each other, they come to appreciate one another more and more.

For example, Miss Daisy gains some insight into Hoke one day when she is planting flowers at the cemetery. She asks him to look for the grave of her friend's husband, and it's then that she learns for the first time that Hoke can't read.

In another scene, Hoke witnesses Southern prejudice against Jews when he drives Miss Daisy to the synagogue, only to learn that the building has been bombed.

As they identify with each other's pain, a sense of mutuality develops in their relationship.

One day it snows in Atlanta. Hoke makes it to work anyway. Daisy's son, Boolie, calls to say the snow should melt by noon and then he'll be by. but Daisy tells him not to worry because Hoke is there. "He's very handy. I'm fine. I don't need a thing in the world."

"Hello?" her son reacts. "Have I got the right number? I never heard you say loving things about Hoke before."

His mother responds, "I didn't say I love him. I said he was handy."

It's not a romance, but there's a beautiful bonding taking place between Hoke and Miss Daisy, two people who are learning to respect each other.

As the play nears its end, Daisy is ninety-seven and she has had to be put in a nursing home. Hoke's eyes are going bad. He's in his mid-eighties and can't drive anymore. He takes a cab now when he visits his former employer.

The final scene is Thanksgiving Day. Boolie and Hoke go to visit Miss Daisy. Boolie goes through the motions of saying all the right things, but spending time with his mother is a duty his heart's not in.

Tired of his small talk, Daisy dismisses him, saying that Hoke came to talk to her, not to him. "Go charm the nurses."

And then just the two converse. There are long pauses between the words.

"How are you?" she asks.

"Doin' the bes' I can," he responds.

"Me too."

Hoke sees a piece of Thanksgiving pie on the table, which Daisy hasn't eaten yet. She tries to pick up her fork, but can't manage it. So Hoke says, "Lemme hep you wid this," and he cuts a small piece of pie with the fork and feeds it to her. She smiles and nods her thanks. It's incredibly touching.

Slowly Daisy enjoys a simple piece of pie because of the kindness of a friend who's not in a hurry. Hoke cuts another piece for her. There's no dialogue, and the lights fade and the play is over.

When the world is tough, it's important to guard one another's self-respect.

FOR DISCUSSION AND REFLECTION

1. Can you recall a time when your self-respect was extremely low? What contributed to those feelings?

2. Who is someone who makes you feel insignificant or unimportant? What does this person do that causes you to respond as you do?

3. Name someone in your church who is good at affirming people's self-worth.

4. Was the doctrine of Creation and the original dignity of men and women emphasized in the church where you grew up? How were you affected by the presence or lack of that emphasis?

5. Explain why guarding self-respect could be an important survival skill during the '90s.

6. Review Philippians 3:4-11. What kind of human credentials are sometimes elevated too much in the church, when really they belong in the rubbish category? What can be done about this?

READINGS

There are some basic flaws in the proposition that spiritual truth is best apprehended by the most mature, most logical, most modern, and most brilliant minds. Such intellectual chauvinism is certainly in conflict with Jesus' admonition to look to the children to find the secrets of the Kingdom: "Thou hast hidden these things from the wise and understanding and revealed them to babes" (Matthew 11:25, RSV).

After Donny's death, Ruth went to work supervising the kitchen and dining-room staff at the Apple Doll House restaurant, a regional program that employs adult retarded citizens. How many parents who lose a child have the privilege to go to work each day and see the same beloved face? Seeing Down's syndrome people each day was a miraculous way to assuage the grief and retain the wonder of the small life that was no longer part of hers. No manager could have loved her employees more than Ruth. . . .

One of Ruth's charges, Mary Kate, excelled as a waitress and was soon promoted to hostess. When I visited, she always served my table despite her exalted new job description. She led an active life outside of work, living in a group home with other adults with Down's syndrome and competing in a variety of sports events.

It was Christmastime when I came for lunch with three guests. While we were contemplating the excellent alternatives on the menu, Mary Kate was in the corner quietly repeating, over and over again, "Croissant, croissant, croissant." The menu was arranged by numbers to simplify things for the staff. One of my guests ordered by number, but Mary Kate was not about to have her rehearsal efforts wasted: "Would that be the ham and cheese *croissant?*"

My guest complimented her on her superb French pronunciation. Mary Kate looked down demurely and said, "Thank you, but my Spanish is so much better than my French." She and Ruth, her Spanish teacher, then treated us to a duet of "Feliz Navidad."

Speech and language do not come easily for persons with Down's syndrome and represent one of their greatest sources of frustration. It takes courage for many who are retarded to risk being understood in their native tongue, let alone a foreign language. Love like Ruth's uses imagination to fuel courage.

The most gripping description of the prophetic role of the Down's syndrome individual is in Morris West's novel, *Clowns of God.* West's vision of Jesus' second coming describes the returned Christ with a Down's child on his knee, serving her eucharistic bread and wine.

> What better [sign] could I give than to make this little one whole and new? I could do it; but I will not. . . . I gave this mite a gift I denied to all of you—eternal innocence. . . . She will never offend me, as all of you have done. She will never pervert or destroy the works of my Father's hands. She is necessary to you. She will evoke the kindness that will keep you human. . . . She will remind you every day that I AM WHO I AM.

Since the overall life expectancy for children with cancer has improved and the life-opportunities for people with Down's syndrome have advanced, more of God's prophetic clowns are with us. Each time I partake of the bread and wine, I am reminded of their kindness and the many ways they keep me human.

A Window to Heaven, Diane M. Komp, Zondervan, pages 58–60.

● ● ●

God Gave Me His Name

I am a light
I am His bride
An heir to His Kingdom
His cross at my side
I am His friend
A son and a saint

Anointed with love and mercy and grace
I will stand tall
And carry no shame
When I remember
God gave me His name.

Looking down at the ground
Shadows around me are all I see
They accuse and abuse
Stealing my value
Whispering lies to me

His name will move mountains
And shake up a kingdom with its power and authority
Though I am poor, though weak and afraid
I'll hold my head high
And remember His name
Is my name.

Christine Wyrtzen
Copyright May 1992
Loveland Music

● ● ●

"July 25th somethin' happen'd. I was a tobarker stemmer—
dat is, I took de tobarker leaf an' tor'd de stem out, an' dey
won't no one in dat fact'ry could beat me at dat work. But dat
mornin' de stems wouldn't come out ter save me, an' I tor'd
up tobarker by de poun' an' flung it un'er de table.

"Fac is, bruthr'n, de darkness uv death wuz in my soul dat
mornin'. My sins was pile' on me like mount'ns; my feet wuz
sinkin' down ter de reguns of despar, an' I felt dat uv all
sinners I wuz de wust. I tho't dat I would die right den, an'
wid what I suppose' wuz my lars' breath I flung up to heav'n
a cry for mercy. Befo' I kno'd it, de light broke; I wuz light as
a feather; my feet wuz on de mount'n; salvation roll' like a
flood through my soul, an' I felt as if I could knock off de
factory roof wid my shouts.

"But I sez to myse'f, 'John Jasper, you gotta hol' still til dinner.' So, I cried, an' laughed, an' tor'd up tobarker, and flung it un'er der table.

"Pres'ntly, I looked up der table an' dar wuz a old man—he love me, and tried hard ter lead me out de darknes'. So I slip roun' ter whar he wuz, an' I sez in his ear, low as I could, 'Hallelujah; my soul is redeemed!' Den I jump back quick ter my work.

"But af'er I once open my mouf it wuz hard ter keep it shet eny mo'. 'Twan' long befo' I looked up der line agin, an' dar wuz a good ol' 'oman dar dat knew all my sorrers an' had been prayin' fer me all de time. Dar wuz no use er talkin'; I had ter tell her, an' so I skip along up quiet as a breeze an' start ter whisper in her ear, but jes' den de holin'-back straps uv Jasper's breechin' broke an' what I tho't would be a whisper wuz loud enuf ter be hearn clean 'cross Jeems river ter Manchester. One man sed he tho't de factory wuz fallin' down. All I know'd wuz I had raise my fus' shout ter de glory uv my Redeemer."

["De holin'-back straps broke" is a good description. In a moment, the factory was filled with Jasper's shouts and the prayerful hallelujahs of Christian friends.]

"But fer one thing thar would er been a jin'ral revival in de fact'ry dat mornin'. Dat one thing wuz de overseer. He bulged inter de room an', wid a voice dat sounded like he had his breakfus' dat mornin' on rasps an' files, bellowed out: 'What's all dis row 'bout?' Somebody shouted out dat John Jasper done got religion. But dat didn't wurk 'tall wid de boss. He tell me ter git back ter my table, an' as he had somethin' in his han' dat look ugly, it wuz no time fer makin' fine p'ints. So I sed: 'Yes, suh, I will; I ain't meant no harm. De fus' taste of salvation got de better uv me, but I'll git back ter my wurk.' An' I tell you I got back quick.

" 'Bout dat time, Marse Sam, he come out'n his orfis an' he say, 'What's de matter out here?' An' I hear de overseer tellin' him 'John Jasper kick up a fuss an' say he done got religion, but I done fix him an' he got back ter his table.'

"De devil tell me ter hate de overseer dat mornin', but de luv uv Gord wuz rolin' through my soul, an' somehow I didn't min' what he sed.

"Little art'r I hear Marse Sam tell de overseer he wan' ter
see Jasper. Marse Sam wuz a good man. He wuz a Baptis', an'
one uv de haid men uv de ole Fus' Church down here. So I
wuz glad wen I hear Marse Sam say he wan' ter see me. Wen
I git in his orfis he say, 'John, wat wuz de matter out dar jes'
now?' His voice wuz sof' like, an' it seem'd ter hav a little
song in it which play inter my soul like an angel's harp. I sez
ter him: 'Marse Sam, did I ever give you eny trouble?'

"He look at me wid water in his eyes, an' he say, 'No,
John, you never did.' Den I broke ter cryin' an' sez ter him:
'Marse Sam, ever since de fourth uv July I been cryin' after
de Lord—an' jes' now, out dar at de table, Gord took my sins
'way an' set my feet on a rock. I didn't mean ter make no
noise, Marse Sam, but befo' I know'd it de fires broke out in
my soul an' I jes' let go one shout ter de glory uv my Savior.'

"Marse Sam wuz settin' wid his eyes a little down ter de
flo', an' wid a pretty quiver in his voice he say very slow:
'John, I b'leve dat way myse'f. I love de Savior dat you have
jes' foun' an' I wan' to tell you dat I do'n complain 'cause you
make de noise you did.'

"Den Marse Sam did a thing dat nearly made me drop ter
de flo'. He git out uv his chair an' walk over ter me an' give
me his han', an' he say: 'John, I wish you mighty well. Your
Savior is mine, an' we are bruthers in de Lord.' Wen he say
dat I turn 'roun an' put my arm agin de wall, an' put my fis' in
my mouf ter keep from shoutin'.

"Marse Sam well know de good he done us. After awhile
he say, 'John, did you tell any uv dem in thar 'bout your
conversion?' An' I say, 'Yes, Marse Sam; I tell 'em befo' I
know'd it, an' I feel like tellin' ever'body in de worl' 'bout it.'
Den he say: 'You may tell it. Go back in dar an' go up an'
down de table en' tell all uv dem. An' den if you wan' to, go
upstars an' tell dem all 'bout it, an' den go downstars an' tell
de hogshead men an' de drivers an' ever'body wat de Lord
has done for you.'

"By dis time Marse Sam's face wuz rainin' tears, an' he
say: 'John, you needn' wurk no mo' terday. I give you holiday.
Af'er you git through tellin' it here at de fact'ry, go up ter de
house an' tell your mother; go roun' ter your neighbors an'

tell dem; go enywhere you wan' ter an' tell de good news. It'll do you good, do dem good, an' help ter honor your Lord an' Savior.'

"Af'er awhile Marse Sam lif' up dem kin' black eyes uv his an' say: 'Keep tellin' it, John! Fly like an angel, John, and wherever you go, tell it!'

"O happy day! Can I ever fergit it? Dat wuz my conversion mornin', an' dat day de Lord sen' me out wid de good news uv de Kingdom. Fer mo' dan sixty years I'se been tellin' de story."

Rhapsody in Black, Richard Ellsworth Day, The Judson Press, pages 56–58.

● ● ●

Consider the mighty ways in which God used a dead stick of wood. "God so used a stick of wood" can be a banner cry for each of us. Though we are limited and weak in talent, physical energy and psychological strength, we are not less than a stick of wood. But as the rod of Moses had to become the rod of God, so that which is *me* must become the *me* of God. Then, I can become useful in God's hands. The Scripture emphasizes that much can come from little if the little is truly consecrated to God. There are no little people and no big people in the true spiritual sense, but only consecrated and unconsecrated people. The problem for each of us is applying this truth to ourselves: Is Francis Schaeffer the Francis Schaeffer of God?

No Little Places
But if a Christian is consecrated, does this mean he will be in a big place instead of a little place? The answer, the next step, is very important: As there are no little people in God's sight, so there are no little places. To be wholly committed to God in the place where God wants him—this is the creature glorified. In my writing and lecturing I put much emphasis on God's being the infinite reference point which integrates the intellectual problems of life. He is to be this, but he must be the reference point not only in our thinking but in our living.

This means being what he wants me to be, where he wants me to be.

Nowhere more than in America are Christians caught in the twentieth-century syndrome of size. Size will show success. If I am consecrated, there will necessarily be large quantities of people, dollars, etc. This is not so. Not only does God not say that size and spiritual power go together, but he even reverses this (especially in the teaching of Jesus) and tells us to be deliberately careful not to choose a place too big for us. We all tend to emphasize big works and big places, but all such emphasis is of the flesh. To think in such terms is simply to hearken back to the old, unconverted, egoist, self-centered *Me*. This attitude, taken from the world, is more dangerous to the Christian than fleshly amusement or practice. It is the flesh.

No Little People, Francis A. Schaeffer, InterVarsity Press, pages 17–18.

Prague, Czechoslovakia
November 26, 1989
"I was ordained a priest," [Maly] said. "But because I signed Charter 77, I had to clean toilets: that's why I'm asking you now for one minute of silence for all the oppressed."

A hush suddenly fell on the boisterous crowd. There was a long silence, and the cold air was so still that those who shut their eyes could hardly believe they were standing in a field filled with half a million people.

After the moment of silence, Vaclav Benda, the political activist imprisoned with Havel, took the stage to read out a list of names of political prisoners just released on orders of the new government. Among the names on the list, Jan Carnogursky, a leading Slovak Catholic and human rights activist, and Father Stefan Javorsky, a sixty-four-year-old Slovak priest. The crowd let out a cheer for every name Benda read. After the last name on the list, they took out their keys and shook them in that CHINK CHINK CHINK CHINK peal that had come to symbolize their clamor for freedom.

The parade of speakers continued, and the protestors responded with the same enthusiasm. As folk singer Jaroslaw Chudka performed, they sang along lustily, swaying, their hands held high in the victory sign. He had just returned to his homeland from a twenty year exile. The crowd knew every word of his songs, despite the regime's ban on his music. The authorities' attempt to enforce "forgetting" had obviously failed.

The crowd was exuberant. They laughed, then cried, for joy. But then a serious note.

Havel led two people forward and Maly introduced them as high-ranking members of the security police responsible for the brutality against the student demonstration the week before. The crowd started jeering.

"They have come to apologize," Maly shouted over the loudspeaker. The crowd fell silent. He could almost sense their desire for revenge.

A tall, good-looking man wearing a fatigue-colored parka stepped forward and looked at the stony faces.

"My name is Ludwig Pinc," he told the crowd. "I'm a lieutenant in the Prague police department. We see that it's a tragedy that we were enlisted to stop the democratic changes now taking place. Most of us joined the public security with the understanding that we would use our power to fight against the criminal element, not to oppress regular working citizens."

The statement elicited cheers from the crowd.

"We share some of the blame for what happened during the last days," he said. "After the unpleasant events on November 17, there's a growing animosity of citizens toward the police. We want to tell you that none of our members had the legal right to use force to suppress the people. But this order didn't come from the police. This was a decision made by the higher-ups in the government."

He was interrupted by jeers. "What lies!" the crowd shouted together.

Maly put up his hands to hush the crowd. The young officer continued facing them, standing stiff and formal. He raised his voice to be heard over the angry chants. "We want to give you our support for the new democratic changes in our country. I want to express our profound apology that our leaders set us against the people of our own country. Last week, the striking students offered their hands to us in friendship. We want to reach out and accept their outstretched hands now."

It was an emotional moment. A few in the audience wiped away tears with their sleeves. One of the other junior officers standing to the side joined his colleague at the podium. He was wearing the red-banded green cap of the security police.

"I just want to add that I hope I never see the day when the people of this country stand against one another."

When the two finished speaking, Maly took the microphone. His face was solemn. The crowd was still.

"We have to be proud of these members of the security police who came forward to apologize," he said. "They could be risking jail for their actions, and we have to protect them. Thank you for your understanding. Whenever there's political change, there's always the danger of the powerless seeking retribution against the powerful. Now, I'm not asking you to forget what those in power have done. But I am asking you to show forgiveness. Forgiveness is more than a word. There's power in forgiveness. There's hope in forgiveness. Now, will you accept their apology?"

There was an ominous silence. Then, a chant commenced, faint at first, but growing louder and louder, until the voice of half a million became one voice.

"We forgive you! We forgive you!"

Maly stood there, tears in his eyes. When the chanting subsided, he said, "I would like to end this special moment with a prayer. Those of you who know the words, I invite you to say them aloud with me. Those of you who don't know the words, pray with me in your hearts."

He began reciting the Lord's Prayer. Some in the audience prayed along, others fumbled for the words, until Letna field rang with the sound of a prayer that no one had dared to utter in public in more than forty years.

Revolution by Candlelight, Bud Bultman, Multnomah, pages 211–213.

CHAPTER SIX
LEARNING OUR LIMITS

The time of the Crusaders certainly qualifies as an era of great change throughout Europe. The term *crusade* comes from the Latin word *crux,* meaning cross. Sanctioned by ecclesiastical inspiration, the purpose of the Crusades was to recapture the Holy Land from the Moslems. Generally speaking, the Crusades were not successful.

Do you remember the stories of Robin Hood in Sherwood Forest? They take place in England during the twelfth century when good King Richard was out of the country leading a crusade.

I recall having just turned forty and seeing a Sean Connery film called *Robin and Marian.* In this story, it was Robin Hood, not King Richard, who returned from the Crusades and found conditions back in England deplorable. He decided that he'd repeat the routine of his earlier years and organize a new merry band of outlaws. The film plot was interesting to me because I was just beginning a new venture myself. God was leading me into a ministry in broadcasting as I entered the decade of my forties. So I felt like cheering when Robin Hood rose to the challenge and conquered the evil Sheriff of Nottingham. But it bothered me that in the story Robin's victory cost him his life. He wasn't a survivor.

One of the unusual features of this film is the way it shows how everything was harder for Robin Hood now that he was older. For example, climbing the wall of a castle left him so exhausted that when he finally got to the top he just stretched out on his back, pooped. The fights went faster because at this age he didn't last as long as he used to. In one escape scene, Robin Hood and a companion leapt from a wall onto a passing hay wagon. The timing was perfect, except that now these two weighed more than they used to, and when they landed in the wagon the wheels collapsed.

It's a funny idea for a story to show someone going back and trying to relive an earlier and more physically fit stage of life. In the real world, every so often a sports star will try to make a comeback—usually unsuccessfully. There aren't many boxers like George Foreman who are well over forty and willing to take the punishment in the ring that he does. After his first retirement, Foreman tried pastoring a church for a while. I can't believe that experience was so difficult it drove a middle-aged man back to prizefighting, but maybe so!

One way or the other, the survival skill I want to explore in this chapter is learning our limits. It's a natural follow-up to guarding self-respect. The foundation for being able to set appropriate limits is proper self-esteem. If we don't know who we are, we may let others cross boundaries that should not be trespassed.

Know Your Limits
In a troubled world of too many needs, it's wise for Christians to know their ministry limits. Being able to help one individual doesn't mean I can help his three friends. Resolving one person's problems doesn't necessarily make me qualified to help everyone who comes to me. Doing a good job serving on a committee doesn't mean I will do well if I'm assigned to two or three more. Just because I played on the church basketball team in my thirties, that doesn't mean my game is still good when I'm in my forties. After ten minutes I could end up flat on my back gasping for air. All of us need to learn our limits.

Even Jesus had to draw the line as to what He could and couldn't do. There's an interesting event recorded in Mark 1. It was early in our Lord's ministry and the crowd's response was outstanding. Verses 32-34 read: "That evening after sunset the people brought to Jesus all the sick and demon-possessed. The whole town gathered at the door, and Jesus healed many who had various diseases. He also drove out many demons."

The disciples knew from past experience that when the fish were biting, that was not the time to look for another spot. So they may have been baffled by what followed.

"Very early in the morning, while it was still dark, Jesus got up, left the house and went off to a solitary place, where He prayed. Simon and his companions went to look for Him, and when they found Him, they exclaimed: 'Everyone is looking for You!' " (vv. 35-37) That seemed to be true. The ranks of those wanting Jesus to touch them with His healing hands had certainly swollen. So the "merry men" in Christ's band said in essence, "Get back to where You just ministered, Jesus. You can't imagine how many people are there, and You're keeping them waiting."

Those of us in ministry know how draining it is to give and give and give and never get to the end of the line of those wanting help. But Jesus wasn't worn out at this time. What He said was (v. 38), "Let us go somewhere else—to the nearby villages—so I can preach there also. That is why I have come."

Many of Christ's followers today get caught up meeting needs that aren't closely related to the primary job God has called them to do. I know people like that. Sometimes their hyperactive schedules keep them so on the run that they can't take time to be alone with their Heavenly Father. They don't get the chance to talk with Him, much less to hear Him whisper to their hearts. Maybe you're that way.

In the early chapters of Acts, we read that the apostles faced this problem. But they had enough sense to correct it. Acts 6 tells about a situation where it seems there were more needs than the apostles had time to meet. The non-Hebrew widows complained that they were being overlooked in the daily food distribution. In effect what the Twelve said was, "Our priorities don't allow us the time to look after this problem." But let me cite their words right from Scripture, beginning with verse 2: "It would not be right for us to neglect the ministry of the Word of God in order to wait on tables. Brothers, choose seven men from among you who are known to be full of the Spirit and wisdom. We will turn this responsibility over to them and will give our attention [take note] to prayer and the ministry of the Word."

That's exactly what the church did. Those chosen were presented to the apostles, "who prayed and laid their hands on them." The result was that (v. 6) "the word of God spread. The number of disciples in Jerusalem increased rapidly" (v. 7).

Do you see how the apostles knew their limits? There was a genuine need, it's true, but the pressure of authentic needs didn't mean the apostles personally had to meet them. That's a lesson they had learned from their Lord. Pitiful people had come from everywhere to be healed by Jesus, but that didn't mean He was obligated to do so. He could, yes, but to double-check whether that's what His Father wanted, He got up early in the morning to spend time with Him.

The disciples applied the same principle in this Acts 6 passage: "We'll turn the food distribution over to seven other capable men so we can give our attention to talking with the Lord [prayer] and to the ministry of the Word."

Seek God's Will

It's probably a good reminder to all of us that when we're so busy we're constantly shortchanging our time in prayer and God's Word, whoever we are we need to make some adjustments. We need to get rid of some of the clutter of our hyperactive lives. Sometimes we have to say words like, "I'm honored that you've asked me to serve and I understand the need you're talking about, but if I help I'll shortchange higher spiritual priorities. So if I disappoint you, please understand that I must say no in order not to disappoint the Lord."

Here's something interesting I've discovered. Because someone feels God has led him or her to ask me to do something, that doesn't necessarily mean I'm supposed to say yes. The reverse is also true. When I sense God directing me to ask someone to do a job, that doesn't automatically mean it's God's will for that man or woman to say OK.

God can direct a congregation to call a pastor and then whisper in that minister's heart to say no to the invitation. The need or the request for help doesn't always indicate God's will.

The medieval Crusades I referred to earlier were a tremendous expenditure of time and money and energy. Some accomplished more than others, but most of the benefits were side effects, such as learning how to make better maps and ships that would eventually aid in the exploration of the new world. The main goal of the Crusaders, to regain the Holy Land from the Moslems, went unrealized.

Some of the Crusades were fiascoes. When King Louis IX of France led the Seventh Crusade, the Turks surrounded his army, and he and his noblemen were freed only after the Christians paid a huge ransom.

The Children's Crusade of 1212 was an utter tragedy. It involved two armies made up of boys and girls, most of whom were age twelve and under. They never reached the Holy Land. Many died of hunger, exposure, or as the result of other hardships. Some were sold as slaves or died at sea.

These events remind us of the dangers of getting too quickly involved in spiritual causes without first spending time talking to the Lord about them. And if possible, it's always wise to consult with other mature believers as well.

Learning our limits. That's an important survival skill. So when you do something well in an area of ministry, be aware that sooner or later other Christians may place expectations on you that go beyond what God has in mind. It's important to stay close to the Lord. Your daily marching orders need to come from him.

A little over a hundred years after the last of the Crusades, there emerged in France the unique personage, Joan of Arc. Like most young women of that time, she could neither read nor write. But apparently she was learned in spiritual matters.

It was a dangerous day to be alive. The Hundred Years' War was in process, and at this time much of France was under English rule. Young Joan, a peasant girl, felt commissioned by heaven to liberate her people. (To grasp the absurdity of such an idea, picture an uneducated American teenage girl asking to be made Commander in Chief of our Armed Forces!) But somehow this young woman began to capture the imagination of the French with her claims that God was directing her.

When Joan eventually had an audience with young Charles VII he decided to test her spiritual powers of perception. So he had one of his noblemen sit on his throne while he lost himself among the others of his court. George Bernard Shaw captures this historic moment in his play *Saint Joan.* Young Joan is brought into the room. She's dressed like a soldier. Her hair is bobbed, which causes the perfumed ladies in waiting to explode in almost uncontrollable laughter. But Joan explains, "I wear it like this because I am a soldier. Where be Dauphin?" (The word *Dauphin* refers to the prince or oldest son of the king. Charles is yet uncrowned.)

Young Bluebeard is pretending to be Charles. He's twenty-five and is sporting the extravagance of a little curled beard dyed blue in this otherwise clean-shaven court. He responds somewhat condescendingly, "You are in the presence of the Dauphin."

Joan looks him over quite carefully while everyone present watches in absolute silence. Then comprehending what's going on, a smile lights up her face. "Coom, Bluebeard:" she chides. "Thou canst not fool me. Where be Dauphin?" And as laughter again breaks out, she looks over the group, makes a dive, grabs Charles by the arm, and drags him forward.

"Gentle little Dauphin," she says, "I am sent to you to drive the English away from Orléans and from France, and to crown you king in the cathedral at Rheims, where all true kings of France are crowned."

Eventually, after more testing Joan was placed in charge of the king's troops. History records that she liberated the besieged city of Orléans in 1429. Before the battle, all the French soldiers were served Communion.

The World Book Encyclopedia says that Joan "defeated the English in four other battles. Twice she was wounded, but each time she recovered and went on fighting. Her orders were those of a military genius. She marched into the city of Rheims, where Charles was crowned King of France, with the Maid of Orléans standing at his side with sword and banner."

Now Joan's work was done and her visions ceased. Her desire was to return to her home. But Charles wouldn't have it. There were many needs in his troubled world. Joan had performed incredibly well. Now further expectations were placed on her. The king convinced her to lead an attack on Paris, which was still under English control. The effort failed and she was wounded again.

Later, after being captured by French allies of the English, Joan was sold to the enemy for 16,000 francs. She was placed in prison and eventually put on trial as a witch and a heretic. Not yet out of her teens, she was burned at the stake, insisting to the very end that her visions and voices had come from heaven.

The story of Joan of Arc is a powerful reminder that we must know our limits and stick by them unless God makes it clear that He has other plans. I was in my fifties before I discovered I needed to set personal boundaries, so I'm not one to be critical of a teenager. But the illustration does prove helpful, especially in a discussion of survival skills.

Accept God's Gifts and Guidance

Allow me to make a slight shift in direction. Learning our limits certainly includes knowing how God has gifted us and staying close to Him for guidance. But it also involves paying attention to those times when we need to receive ministry from others. We can't always be giving. Some people never notice when their spiritual gas gauge is on empty. That's a precarious position to be in.

Our Lord is such a help by way of example. Mark 14:3-9 records the incident where Christ was dining at the home of Simon the Leper in Bethany. It was the final week of our Lord's life. Knowing what was ahead, He must have been under great stress. Then a woman came with an alabaster jar of expensive perfume, which was worth a year's wages for the average worker. She had brought something of real value. (If a person came to you with a gift that you knew cost an entire year's salary, you'd be impressed!) The woman broke the jar and poured the perfume on Jesus' head.

It was as if she was saying, "Gentle prince, Dauphin, Son of the Most High, I have been sent to anoint You in the manner of all true kings."

Almost immediately the woman was criticized for her actions by some of the dinner guests. Verses 4-5 tell us, "Some of those present were saying indignantly to one another, 'Why this waste of perfume? It could have been sold for more than a year's wages and the money given to the poor.' And they rebuked her harshly." To be rebuked for giving a costly gift was hard enough, but she was rebuked harshly.

"Leave her alone." Those are Jesus' words. "Why are you bothering her?" Their faultfinding was out of line.

"She has done a beautiful thing to Me," He continued. "The poor you will always have with you, and you can help them any time you want. But you will not always have Me."

So he defended the woman, but there was an obvious touch of gratitude in His words also. She understood what was happening. She was one of the few who did. When Jesus told those present at the dinner, "You will not always have Me," He knew His words would become reality within days. He said specifically, "She poured perfume on My body beforehand to prepare for My burial."

Good for her.

And good for our Lord that He was aware that such a marvelous gesture of love could be received, that it was not a gift that was out of line, that it was appropriate and timely and God-directed. It was from an unnamed woman, yes, but it was also a gift from His Father, who used this woman-servant to carry His message: "You're a special Son worth everything in the world to Me. I understand that what You're facing is extremely difficult. Don't wobble, walk tall. You're not alone. You're loved."

Some people can minister, but they can't be ministered to. They try to outdo Jesus. That's not easy and it's not necessary.

I know Christians with a servant mind-set who know that their Master can give tough assignments. But they seem unfamiliar with the fact that He also *occasionally* likes to reach out in special ways and affirm those who selflessly serve Him.

Don't confuse what I'm saying with the message of those who preach that following Christ means living the good life:

owning several houses that rival palaces, driving luxury cars (plural), wearing the finest clothes, and eating out all the time at gourmet restaurants.

What I'm saying is that *occasionally* God will say to those on the front lines, "Take a break and enjoy a surprise I have for you. I've arranged for one of My servants to open his summer home for you and provide a nice car for you to drive. He'll make available what would seem to cost you a year's salary if you tried to do it on your own, but it's a gift. Enjoy it."

Some people don't know how to receive such an offer and say thank You to God. They only know how to work until they drop. Maybe they won't survive as long as their Master intended.

So one of the most important survival skills we can master is to learn our limits. We need to recognize when we've been pushing too hard for too long, when it's time for a well-deserved break.

In this regard being Christlike occasionally involves letting the Father overwhelm us by showing His love through material gifts that could be as outlandish as an incredibly expensive bottle of perfume.

FOR DISCUSSION AND REFLECTION

1. What are ways to differentiate between a challenge the Lord has set before you and a request that would violate your limits?

2. Would people say you are someone who knows how to minister but not how to be ministered to? Why or why not?

3. It is inevitable that some of our learning about limits will come through trial and error. What is good and what is bad about this method?

4. Name various reasons pastors might sometimes be insensitive to the limits of their parishoners.

5. When might learning your limits literally be a survival skill?

6. What are some passages in the Bible that deal with the matter of learning our limits? (example: Ex. 18)

READINGS

Gandhi's spinning wheel was his center of gravity in life. It was the great leveler in his human experience. When he returned from the great public moments in his life, the spinning-wheel experience restored him to his proper sense of proportion, so that he was not falsely swelled with pride due to the cheers of the people. When he withdrew from the moments of encounter with kings and government leaders, he was not tempted to think of himself in some inflated fashion when he moved to the work of the wheel.

The spinning wheel was always a reminder to Gandhi of who he was and what the practical things in life were all about. In engaging in this regular exercise, he was resisting all the forces of his public world that tried to distort who he knew himself to be.

Gandhi was by no means a Christian, but what he was doing at the wheel is an indispensable lesson for any healthy Christian. For he shows us what every man or woman who wants to move in a public world without being pressed into its mold needs to do. We, too, need the spinning-wheel experience—the ordering of our private worlds so that they are constantly restructured in strength and vitality.

As Thomas Kelly says, "We are trying to be several selves at once, without all our selves being organized by a single, mastering Life within us." Again he says, "Life is meant to be lived from a Center, a divine Center. Each one of us can live such a life of amazing power and peace and serenity, of integration and confidence and simplified multiplicity, on one condition—that is, *if we really want to.*"

And that is the condition with which we must finally deal. Do we really want order within our private worlds? Again, *do we want it?*

If it is true that actions speak louder than words, it would appear that the average Christian does not really seek an ordered private world as a top priority. It would seem that we prefer to find our human effectiveness through busyness, frantic programming, material accumulation, and rushing to various conferences, seminars, film series, and special speakers.

In short, we try to bring order to the inner world by beginning with activity in the outer one. This is exactly the opposite of what the Bible teaches us, what the great saints have shown us, and what our dismal spiritual experiences regularly prove to us.

Somewhere John Wesley is quoted as saying of life in his public world, "Though I am always in haste, I am never in a hurry, because I never undertake more work than I can go through with calmness of spirit."

Ordering Your Private World, Gordon MacDonald, Oliver Nelson, pages 178–179.

● ● ●

Sometimes Christians choose to fight insignificant matters. A friend was once involved in a public dispute with (believe it or not) a bakery selling "pornographic cookies." I agreed with him in the sense that the bakery shouldn't do that. But if a simple conversation with the owner didn't work, it would probably only end up as a waste of time and a source of embarrassment.

A well-known Christian legal organization once filed a "friend of the court" brief supporting a man from Virginia who wanted to have the word "atheist" on his license plate. They did so because it was a matter of religious freedom. Even though they were probably right as a matter of abstract constitutional law, I believe that it was a waste of time and money to write, print, and file the brief. There are so many important battles out there, why get involved with the atheists and license plates?

Frankly, I don't like to be confronted with *National Enquirer* or *Star* magazines at grocery store checkout lines with headlines about "sex nymphs," "Elvis reincarnated," or "crystal power." But other than expressing my opinion to the store manager, there is little I can do that is likely to be effective. I want to spend my time taking on issues that count.

Actually, this is a very good way to determine whether a particular organization is worth supporting. Ask yourself: What are they spending their time and money to accomplish? If they are going to fight homosexuality by sending petitions to the President," save your money. The President seldom reads petitions, and one on the general issue of homosexuality will have no effect whatsoever on public policy. If there is a bill pending in Congress concerning gay rights, then by all means write to the President and to Congress. But generalized concerns about abstract problems do not make a lot of difference.

A series of questions will help you pick out battles that count.

● Will my action help advance a long-range objective of importance to me?

● Is there any chance that I can succeed?

● Is there some other project I could choose that would more effectively advance the same goal?

Don't limit yourself to working on an issue only when you know you can win. It is just as important to stand up for what's right, even if you don't believe you can win. But don't waste your time on an issue that would not be of significance even if you did win. You should make sure that the time, effort, and money you spend on a project bears some reasonable relation to the importance of the potential victory.

There is one issue that has consumed an enormous amount of Christian's time and resources over the years, and I believe it needs closer examination. That issue is prayer in the public schools. The Supreme Court decision that banned prayer in schools was issued in 1962. That is fully three decades ago. While Christians have focused enormous resources working to reverse that decision, the secularists have changed the entire face of the public school system through values clarification, evolution, permissive sex education, and other programs that focus on the five-hours-and-fifty-nine minutes that follow the opening one minute of the school day.

We have to ask ourselves if a minute of prayer—prayer that is likely to be so watered down as to be of questionable value—is worth the effort, especially in light of the energy that could be spent on issues that have a greater chance of success. It is very hard to reverse a decision of the Supreme Court. In fact, there are only two ways to reverse a Supreme Court decision: through Congress, either by legislation or a constitutional amendment; or by getting new justices on the Supreme Court. All other efforts are a waste of time. However, a decision to implement sex education or values clarification is usually made by a school board. It is much easier to have a significant impact on such decisions.

Pick a battle that will mean something to you and your family both *now* and in the *future*. Use as your weapon the effectiveness of focusing on a goal that is worth the time and effort.

Where Do I Draw the Line? Michael P. Farris, pages 39–41.

● ● ●

Very important in letting go of control is to affirm that God is the true Messiah. We can do this in two ways. First, we can stop acting like we are the messiah. We have to scrutinize any action we take to "help" our families. Perhaps we hear of a new program or a counselor in their area. We rush to the phone to tell them about it. Or perhaps we meet a dynamic person who lives in their town. "If only Joe could meet my father, I know my father would respond to him and get help." We begin to scheme and orchestrate. Now how could I get Joe to talk with my father?

Watch out when this happens. It is easy for us to rationalize sending another in our place to save our families.

Second, we can start affirming that Jesus is the only true Savior for our lives or the lives of our families. John the Baptist had a strong ministry to proclaim the coming of the Messiah, but he realized that when the Messiah, Jesus, did come, it would be time for his own ministry to fade away. "He must increase, but I must decrease" (John 3:30). The same thing must happen in our own lives. We must consciously affirm that God is the only one with the plan of salvation for our parent or any other person we desire to see helped.

As part of this process, we need to learn to establish new boundaries in our family relationships. Before, it was confusing where we began and our parents ended. Our families came to expect us to be there for them. In an odd way, the abusive parent came to depend on our willingness to "just take it" when he dished out his blows—verbal or otherwise.

Now we must learn to establish boundaries and set limits on the behavior of others. "No, you can't do that to me." "No, that is not a proper way to talk to me." These are new concepts for us and can be very frightening. Sometimes we may need help establishing these boundaries.

On May 30, 1975, a week before my college graduation, I wrote in my journal, "God, please, only You can do this. Please help Dad be glad, not mad, at my graduation. Oh Lord, I am scared because I feel so out of place with my family. Everyone else will be hugging and happy and glad to be with their families. I am so afraid my father will fight, make a scene, and ruin it somehow for me. I am afraid I will feel very, very lonely. Please, God, I need Your help."

My worst fears came to pass. My father came to the baccalaureate service that bright June morning of graduation day with a heavy scowl on his face. He was angry and I didn't know why. "Please, God, please don't let him make a scene. Not today!"

I introduced him to my friend's parents, Reverend and Mrs. Woodward, who had taken me into their home for many Christmases and holidays. He snapped at them and turned and walked off. I stood there horrified. I made a hurried apology and ran after him. We stood in the quadrangle and talked.

"Your mother was a demanding woman," he snapped. "I could never satisfy her. All she wanted was money. And for what? To send you kids to college so you could parade around in some cap and gown and think you know everything? Well, let me tell you something, young lady, you don't know nothing. I've had the school of hard knocks teach me a few things, but you're just full of book knowledge. You've got a lot to learn, and I can't wait to see you get your comeuppance."

I was in tears. The quadrangle was filled with activity as families walked back from the baccalaureate service. Suddenly, out of the corner of my eye, I spotted a professor, Mary Boney Sheats, coming toward us. "Oh, no," I thought. "Please, Dad, be nice to her." Dr. Sheats had known my mother and was coming to greet my father. He snarled at her in the same hangdog way. I was mortified. In absolute graciousness, she wished my father well and then pulled me aside. With her hands on my shoulders, she looked deeply into my eyes and said, "Nancy, this is your day. Do not let him ruin it for you. You have worked hard for this, and you deserve to enjoy it. Now tell him to go home, get himself together, and you'll expect him not to come back for the graduation service unless he can act responsibly."

I looked up at her in surprise. What she was telling me to tell my father seemed so authoritative and so presumptuous. Somehow, I did exactly what she said, perhaps because of the strength of the peace in her eyes. No one was more surprised than I when he reappeared at 5:00 P.M., as civil as anyone could be.

This was my first taste of setting boundaries. I needed more practice, however; and under the guidance of my counselor, I began to establish new boundaries for my relationship with my father.

No Longer the Hero, Nancy LeSourd, Thomas Nelson, pages 174–177.

● ● ●

CINDY: Working together as we did in Africa was a total high for me. We'd walk back from teaching a class at the college — at least half a mile on dirt roads — and we would just laugh and laugh. It was so wonderful.

We had lots of time to talk. Too many couples just don't do that it seems. Jim would come home everyday at lunch and for a whole hour we might sit on the porch together. We would literally sit in the rocking chairs and talk about us, our relationship. We reflected on the past. We looked forward to the future. We talked about the pitfalls we saw in our relationship and what to do about them. Most importantly, we made some decisions about the pace of our life once we returned home. We consciously decided—before coming back—to downscale our stress levels.

JIM: During that year away I also came to understand that, professionally, I needed to set some limits in terms of personal involvement with patient problems. Especially if I wanted to survive practicing medicine! Oh, I'm still a good listener. I continue to care deeply about my patients and give each one focused attention; but when I go home, I'm learning not to ruminate on all the extra "baggage" in some of their lives. I'm no longer internalizing it. I'm not churning on it for hours and hours. So this is really helping me not to pay such a high emotional cost in my medical practice. But it wasn't until I stepped back for a while that I realized what a significant price I had been paying personally.

As a doctor, my tendency has always been to feel responsible for other people's lives and the decisions they make. Now, instead, I'm much more inclined to approach people with the attitude, "I'm going to be positive and give my honest input when permitted, and then stand back and leave it to God." It's a major growth edge for me. It's a practical way I can rehearse the truth that "God's in control," not me.

Coming Back, Steve and Valerie Bell, Victor Books, page 90.

● ● ●

In speaking with pastors of declining churches, a common thread was their desire to do something for everybody. They had fallen into the strategic black hole of creating a ministry that looked great on paper, but had no ability to perform up to standards. Despite their worthy intentions, they tried to be so helpful to everyone that they wound up being helpful to no one. Their laudable objectives and resulting frustrations were evident in the words of one of the pastor[s] who said, "I just don't understand it. My only desire is to serve Him. I do my best to be there for everyone. Nothing seems to have a lasting impact, though. Our numbers are declining, our impact in the community is virtually nil. It just doesn't make sense."

In a world filled with hurting people, we want to be the solution. Having been touched by the love of Christ in our own lives, it is only natural that we want to return the favor by sharing that love with others by being the answer to their every need. As a church, we are anxious to be on the spot, sharing the love of Christ and the truth of the gospel with everyone. The temptation is to try to satisfy every need that people can identify.

A Specific Mission

Even the growing, healthy churches I studied frequently struggle with this concept. Believe me, it is even more tempting to try to provide one-stop spiritual shopping when your church has had an unbroken string of successes.

However, the stark reality is that every church has limited resources, and has been called to accomplish a specific mission. Despite the urge to be all things to all people, the successful churches resisted that impulse to be the answer to everyone's every problem by focusing on their vision for ministry, by reaffirming their commitment to quality, and by recognizing their limitations. If they were to devote themselves to meeting every need in their marketplace, they would dissipate their resources and have no impact—the very tragedy that has befallen the majority of the Protestant churches in America. In general, these growing congregations refused to be enticed into areas of ministry in which they discerned no special calling. Instead, they concentrated on doing what they knew, beyond a doubt, they were called to do.

User Friendly Churches, George Barna, Regal, pages 50–52.

CHAPTER SEVEN
APPRECIATING WHAT SUFFERING TEACHES

The Chosen, by Chaim Potok, is one of my favorite stories. Published as a book twenty-five years ago, it was made into a feature film about fifteen years late.

It's a modern story about two young men, both Jewish, growing up in New York City. It begins during the final years of World War II and continues through the time of the founding of the modern state of Israel.

Daniel is a Hasidic, or very strict, Jew. He wears the earlocks and the plain black clothes of his people. Daniel's father is the head of the local synagogue.

Danny is an incredible young man. His mind is sharp. He has a photographic memory. He's a strong and superior athlete. But for some unknown reason, his father won't talk to him except in religion classes. He speaks in a fatherly way to his other children, but not to Danny.

Reuven, Danny's friend, tells the story. He is a Reformed Jew.

This strange silence of a father toward his son plays itself out through the entire book. It's not until the end when Danny and Reuven are nearing college graduation, that the reason is revealed.

The two young men sit in Danny's father's third floor study. The older man talks to Reuven, but his words are meant for Daniel, to whom he doesn't speak. And now the truth comes out.

Reuven, the Master of the Universe blessed me with a brilliant son. And he cursed me with all the problems of raising him. Ah, what it is to have a brilliant son! Not a

smart son, Reuven, but a brilliant son, a Daniel, a boy
with a mind like a jewel.... Reuven, when my Daniel
was four years old, I saw him reading a story from a
book. And I was frightened. He did not read the story,
he swallowed it, as one swallows food or water. There
was no soul in my four-year-old Daniel, there was only
his mind. He was a mind in a body without a soul. It was
a story in a Yiddish book about a poor Jew and his
struggles to get to Eretz Yisroel before he died. Ah, how
that man suffered! And my Daniel *enjoyed* the story, he
enjoyed the last terrible page, because when he finished
it he realized for the first time what a memory he had.
He looked at me proudly and told me back the story
from memory, and I cried inside my heart. I went away
and cried to the Master of the Universe, "What have
you done to me? A mind like this I need for a son? A
heart I need for a son, a *soul* I need for a son, *compassion*
I want from my son, righteousness, mercy, strength to
suffer and carry pain, *that* I want from my son, not a
mind without a soul!"

Reuven continues his description of this momentous meeting:

Reb Saunders [Daniel's father] paused and took a deep,
trembling breath. I tried to swallow; my mouth was
sand-dry. Danny sat with his right hand over his eyes,
his glasses pushed up on his forehead. He was crying
silently, his shoulders quivering. Reb Saunders did not
look at him.

"...Better I should have had no son at all than to
have a brilliant son who had no soul. I looked at my
Daniel when he was four years old, and I said to myself,
How will I teach this mind what it is to have a soul?
How will I teach this mind to understand pain? How will
I teach it to *want* to take on another person's suffering?
How will I do this and not lose my son, my precious son
whom I love as I love the Master of the Universe
Himself? ..."

He closed his eyes and seemed to shrink into himself.

His hands trembled. He was silent for a long time. Tears rolled slowly down alongside the bridge of his nose and disappeared into his beard. A shuddering sigh filled the room. Then he opened his eyes and stared down at the closed Talmud on the desk. "Ah, what a price to pay. . . . The years when he was a child and I loved him and talked with him and held him under my tallis when I prayed. . . . 'Why do you cry, Father?' he asked me once under the tallis. 'Because people are suffering,' I told him. He could not understand. Ah, what it is to be a mind without a soul, what ugliness it is. . . . Those were the years he learned to trust me and love me. . . . And when he was older, the years I drew myself away from him. . . . 'Why have you stopped answering my questions, Father?' he asked me once. 'You are old enough to look into your own soul for the answers,' I told him. He laughed once and said, 'That man is such an ignoramus Father.' I was angry. 'Look into his soul,' I said. 'Stand inside his soul and see the world through his eyes. You will know the pain he feels because of his ignorance, and you will not laugh.' He was bewildered and hurt. The nightmares he began to have. . . . But he learned to find answers for himself. He suffered and learned to listen to the suffering of others. In the silence between us, he began to hear the world crying. . . .

"You think I was cruel? Yes, I see from your eyes that you think I was cruel to my Daniel. Perhaps. But he has learned."

God Wants Us to Understand

Often in the most difficult of times, it seems as if our Heavenly Father is strangely silent. I have come to believe this is a gift. God wants His people to understand how much His world is in pain. He wants us to identify with the suffering that surrounds us.

This is an extremely difficult lesson to learn in a setting where we're used to having things more or less our own way. Our expectations and our sense of entitlement are high, and our tolerance for others and their problems is usually low.

But God doesn't need men and women working for His cause who have brilliant minds but hard and shriveled souls. He's not necessarily searching for beautiful people, not talented and educated people to be His servants. What He needs is believers who know what it is to be broken.

Pain and suffering can teach a proud person humility and compassion for others. On the other hand, hard times can make a man or woman bitter and resentful.

Paul writes to the Romans, "We know that suffering produces perseverance; perseverance, character: and character, hope" (Rom. 5:3-4). Have you not found that to be true? That some of life's most valuable insights are discovered during difficult times?

The same principle might be applied to a nation. In the Old Testament, Israel seemed to learn better during the hard years than during the good years. This seems to be the case today in places such as the former Soviet Union. It's a difficult time, but oh, the lessons she's learning.

Maybe before too long, we in North America also will experience a drastic change in lifestyle. To prepare us for that time, a key survival skill is to start seeing beyond the pain of suffering, to realize that it could be a gift from a loving Father. When your path is marked by suffering, learn to appreciate the lessons it can teach you.

I walked a mile with Pleasure;
   She chattered all the way,
But left me none the wiser
   For all she had to say.

I walked a mile with Sorrow
   And ne'er a word said she;
But oh, the things I learned from her
   When Sorrow walked with me!

("Along the Road" by Robert Browning Hamilton)

The Apostle Paul was a man who walked many miles with Lady Suffering. Yet he remained true to his Lord. He was a spiritual survivor. He writes in 2 Corinthians 1:3-5:

> Praise be to the God and Father of our Lord Jesus
> Christ, the Father of compassion and the God of all
> comfort, who comforts us in all our troubles, so that we
> can comfort those in any trouble with the comfort we
> ourselves have received from God. For just as the
> sufferings of Christ flow over into our lives, so also
> through Christ our comfort overflows.

Looking back on your experiences, have you sensed God's
comfort during times of sorrow and grief? The great majority
of Christians would respond yes.

That's not to say there was no pain. It doesn't mean your
faith wasn't severely tested. The word *survival* would have
little meaning if your experience were not threatening to
some degree. But you knew God was there. His strength
proved itself adequate. You honestly aren't sure that you
would have made it without the Lord.

Be There for Others

Paul is saying in the Corinthians passage that as God was
there for you in your distress, you can be there for others.
That's one of the great lessons suffering teaches us: to be
considerate of the pain many, many people have to bear.

I had often heard of Alzheimer's disease. I'd talked with
people who told me of family members struggling to cope
with the malady. But several years ago when the disease
touched my mother, I became much more aware of the pain it
inflicts on families. Now when my dad cries as he talks about
Mom's condition, those tears touch me, as does my own
experience of seeing Mom several times each week. I have a
sensitivity I didn't have before.

Paul's second letter to the Corinthians tells of another lesson suffering can teach us. In 2 Corinthians 4:17-18 we learn
that difficult times take our eyes off the temporal and focus
them on the eternal. When suffering, we're reminded of our
mortality. Consequently we're not nearly as concerned about
the things of this world as we are about the life to come.

Paul expresses it this way: "For our light and momentary

troubles are achieving for us an eternal glory that far out-weighs them all. So we fix our eyes not on what is seen, but on what is unseen. For what is seen is temporary, but what is unseen is eternal."

Anyone with a life-threatening disease quickly learns that lesson. This world really isn't our home, we're just passing through. It's easy to get caught up with accumulating a lot of stuff in the process, and to forget that this life is short, compared to that which is to come. Sometimes it takes a close call to bring to mind this truth: "Only one life, t'will soon be past, only what's done for Christ will last." Can we learn to say, "Thank you, Lady Suffering, for the reminder?"

The play, *A Man for All Seasons,* by Robert Bolt, shows how one historical figure got caught in the conflict between this world and the world to come. The main character is Sir Thomas More, who was probably the most brilliant scholar of his day. He entertained in his home such prominent people as Erasmus, Colet, and Holbein. More corresponded with the greatest minds in all of Europe. Though he had an intellect like the Apostle Paul's, More was also a family man, wonderfully humorous and greatly admired, a skilled lawyer who had been knighted by his English government.

The play revolves around More's refusal to take the Oath of Supremacy in 1534, in which Parliament acknowledged Henry VIII as the only Supreme Head on earth of the Church of England. The oath was especially distasteful to More, a Catholic, because it was in reaction to the Pope's unwillingness to grant Henry a divorce. The king had wished to be released from his marriage to Catherine of Aragon so that he could take Anne Boleyn for his wife.

In the play we see Henry desperately seeking More's influential endorsement. More attempts not to commit himself either way. He feels caught between pleasing his God or pleasing his king. Brilliantly he tries to outmaneuver Henry and refrain from taking the oath. Sir Thomas More wants to be a survivor, but it's not going to be easy. The drama captures well the chess-like game played between the monarch and his subject.

Toward the end of the production there's a gripping scene.

More has been in prison for a number of months. His cell is damp and uncomfortable. One day he's surprised by a visit from some of his family. His wife, daughter Margaret, and son-in-law are allowed to see him on the condition that they attempt to convince him to take the Oath of Supremacy. Thomas More quickly discovers what's going on and says to his daughter, "You want me to swear to the Act of Succession?"

Margaret responds, " 'God more regards the thoughts of the heart than the words of the mouth.' Or so you've always told me."

"Yes," More answers.

"Then say the words of the oath and in your heart think otherwise."

But, her father counters, "What is an oath then but words we say to God."

Margaret's somewhat frustrated reply is, "That's very neat."

More attempts to reason, "Do you mean it isn't true?"

"No," she says, "it's true."

"Then it's a poor argument to call it 'neat' Meg," he gently chides her. Then trying somehow to put into words all he's feeling, More says, "When a man takes an oath, Meg, he's holding his own self in his own hands. Like water. [*He cups his hands*] And if he opens his fingers *then* — he needn't hope to find himself again. Some men aren't capable of this, but I'd be loathe to think your father one of them."

At that point Margaret knows he can't do what she's asking, even if by doing so he could return home to those he loves — and save his own life. His relationship with the eternal God is more important to him.

In fact, in the final courtroom scene which follows, More is betrayed by a witness who had been a friend, Richard Rich. At the conclusion of his testimony, Rich begins to leave, but Sir Thomas speaks up. "I have a question to ask the witness. That's a chain of office you are wearing. May I see it? [*He looks at the medallion.*] The red dragon. What's this?"

The answer given is that Sir Richard has been appointed Attorney-General for Wales. More looks into Rich's face with pain and some humor. "For Wales? Why, Richard, it profits a man nothing to give his soul for the whole world . . . but for Wales!"

There's that idea again. Don't fix your eyes on what is seen, but on what is unseen.

Of course the greatest example of this kind of thinking is our Lord. Peter writes about Him this way:

> But how is it to your credit if you receive a beating for doing wrong and endure it? But if you suffer for doing good and you endure it, this is commendable before God. To this you were called, because Christ suffered for you, leaving you an example, that you should follow His steps.
> "He committed no sin, and no deceit was found in His mouth."
> When they hurled their insults at Him, He did not retaliate; when He suffered, He made no threats. Instead, He entrusted Himself to Him who judges justly (1 Peter 2:20-23).

This is exactly what Jesus did: He entrusted Himself to His Father and let Him see to it that the end result was right.

When you receive a "beating" you don't deserve, allow this suffering to teach you to be more Christlike, to identify more closely with what He went through on your behalf, and to appreciate even more the miracle of His love.

Peter gives one final reason to learn to appreciate the lessons of suffering. Remember that his words were written to people being persecuted for their faith. In America we know almost nothing of this.

"Dear friends, do not be surprised at the painful trial you are suffering, as though something strange were happening to you. But rejoice that you participate in the sufferings of Christ, so that you may be overjoyed when His glory is revealed" (4:12-13). Did you catch it? "That you may be overjoyed when His glory is revealed."

There's a lot in this world that isn't fair, that doesn't make sense, that ends without a satisfying resolution, that issues the wrong verdict. These all make us anticipate with joy the revealing of Christ's glory. That's when all will be made right. Suffering encourages us to keep our eyes fixed on that day. Peter continues:

"If you are insulted because of the name of Christ, you are blessed, for the Spirit of glory and of God rests on you. . . . So then, those who suffer according to God's will should commit themselves to their faithful Creator and continue to do good" (vv. 14, 19).

I feel as though I've barely broached this topic of learning through suffering. But even in this short space I trust I've made you aware that you may be holding a precious survival skill in your hands and not know it. Don't let it slip too quickly through your fingers.

When your path is marked by suffering, which happens often in a rapidly changing world, learn to appreciate the lessons pain can teach you. And as we approach the end times and see even more change, let us look with anticipation to the glorious return of our Lord.

FOR DISCUSSION AND REFLECTION

1.   What is a valuable lesson you have learned through sorrow?

2.   Many people become bitter when suffering marks their lives. What determines a person's response?

3.   Can entire congregations learn lessons during difficult times? What determines whether or not this happens?

4.   Nations experience revival more frequently during hard times than they do when all is going well. Why do you think this is?

5.   For what reasons might learning to appreciate the lessons of suffering qualify as a key survival skill?

6.   "Sharing in His sufferings" is a phrase that comes up several times in the New Testament. In what ways do you feel you have shared the sufferings of Christ?

READINGS

Pain itself, the hurt of pain, is a gift. After years of working with lepers, Dr. Paul Brand learned to exult in the sensation of cutting a finger, turning an ankle, stepping into a too-hot bath. "Thank God for pain!" he says.

Doctors once believed the disease of leprosy caused the ulcers on hands and feet and face which eventually led to rotting flesh and the gradual loss of limbs. Mainly through Dr. Brand's research, it has been established that in 99% of the cases, leprosy only *numbs* the extremities. The decay of flesh occurs solely because the warning system of pain is absent.

How does the decay happen? Some villages in Africa and Asia have a unique job for the town leper: he stands by the heavy iron cooking pot watching the potatoes. As they are done, without flinching, he thrusts his arm deep into the scalding water and recovers the cooked potatoes.

Dr. Brand found that abusive acts such as this were the chief cause of body deterioration in the leper. The potato-watching leper had felt no pain, but his skin blistered, his cells were destroyed and laid open to infection. Leprosy had not destroyed the tissue; it had merely removed the warning sensors which alerted the leper to danger.

On one occasion, as Dr. Brand was still formulating this radical theory, he tried to open the door of a little storeroom, but a rusty padlock would not yield to his pressure on the key. A patient, an undersized, malnourished ten-year-old, approached him, smiling.

"Let me try, Sahib doctor," he offered and reached for the key. He closed his thumb and forefinger on the key and with a quick jerk of the hand turned it in the lock.

Brand was dumbfounded. How could this weak youngster out-exert him. His eye caught a telltale clue. Was that a drop of blood on the floor?

Upon examining the boy's fingers, Brand discovered the act of turning the key had slashed the finger open to the bone; skin and fat and joint were all exposed. Yet the boy was completely unaware of it!

The daily routines of life ground away at these lepers' hands and feet, but without a warning system to alert them, they succumbed. If an ankle turned, tearing tendon and muscle, they would adjust and walk crooked. If a rat chewed off a finger in the night, they would not discover it until the next morning.

The discovery revolutionized medicine's approach to leprosy. And it starkly illustrates why Paul Brand can say with utter sincerity, "Thank God for pain!" By definition, pain is unpleasant, so unpleasant as to *force* us to withdraw our finger from a stove, lightning-fast. Yet it is that very quality which saves us from destruction. Unless the warning signal demands response, we might not heed it.

Brand's discovery in the physical realm closely parallels the moral argument for pain offered by C.S. Lewis in *The Problem of Pain*. Just as physical pain is an early warning system to the brain, it is a warning system to the soul. Pain is a megaphone of God which, sometimes murmuring, sometimes shouting, reminds us that something is wrong. It is a "rumor of transcendence," which convinces us the entire human condition is out of whack. We on earth are a rebel fortress, and every sting, and every ache reminds us.

Without pain, we would contentedly build our kingdom of self-sufficiency and pride, professing not to need God (didn't Adam?). Pain removes that privilege. It proves to us that reality is not the way it was meant to be. Something is wrong with a life of wars and screams and insults. We need help.

If you once doubt the megaphone value of pain, visit the intensive care unit of a hospital. In the face of extreme suffering, the human masks are stripped off. Nothing else is important. Blue collar, white collar, black, white, male, female, beautiful, ugly, brilliant, stupid—those status games don't matter in Intensive Care. What matters is life and death. Pain—and only pain—can shout loud enough to bring us to that point.

The Reformed Journal, "In Defense of Pain," Philip Yancey, November 1975.

● ● ●

My amputation showed me the unbalanced emphasis our society puts on our physical bodies. Many of my friends thought that if they were in my shoes—or shoe, I should say—they would have withdrawn. Girlfriends on my track team asked, "Becki, since you were so athletic, how can you have your leg taken away and not be angry?"

I responded, "Well, sure, I loved having two legs, but that's not the most important thing to me. If anything, my body often distracted me. Now it's easier to see that what truly matters is my relationship with God, how I'm living and who I'm loving."

Many of my friends knew I was a Christian. They also knew my dad was a pastor, which in itself was sort of a stigma. But I let my friends know that my beliefs were my own and not imposed by my dad. They knew that church and Campus Life were also important to me.

Some of my friends had ignored the spiritual side of me because they weren't Christians. After I lost my leg, they began to say, "You're different. Why aren't you reacting to your amputation like I would?"

Finally, they listened as I told them about my faith in Jesus Christ and that I was living for something much more lasting than what I was physically. "My relationship with Christ gives me a higher purpose than just what I could accomplish with my physical body," I said. "After all, I have given my life to God; it was really *His* leg that was lost, not mine."

I knew God had answered prayers for my healing. He *had* healed me—emotionally. Incredibly, I never experienced serious depression or anger over my amputation. Incredible to me and unbelievable to everyone else! Only my family and close friends knew I wasn't acting. People, from the very first day, tried to talk me into anger or tell me I was in denial. People urged me to "get in touch with my feelings." I was—and my feelings were fine!

I know this attitude was God's doing, because I know myself! I don't usually say, "O.K. Praise the Lord, and pass the potatoes!" I'm not a hokey Christian whose frothy faith glides me through any circumstance. I usually give God a fight or at least a quiz before I yield to His ultimate power and authority. This was an extraordinary reaction from me, but God never told us life with Him would be ordinary.

Shortly after my surgery, I had to choose a book for an English-class report. Since I had been impressed by Joni when I met her in person, I decided to read her book. Her attitudes strongly molded the way I dealt with my disability. I remember thinking, "I can learn from her times of anger and depression so that maybe I won't go through all of that. Maybe I can skip to be where her life was at the end of the book when she could see God using her disability. I want this amputation to be something positive."

I realized my disability could by no means compare to her quadriplegia, which affects much more of life than an amputation. But I saw that her attitudes applied to my situation. Her life dramatically affected mine, especially in how she wanted to praise the Lord by everything she did.

What God Gives When Life Takes, Becki Conway Sanders, Jim & Sally Conway, InterVarsity Press, pages 90–92.

● ● ●

I beheld, then, that they all went on till they came to the foot of the hill Difficulty, at the bottom of which was a spring. There were also in the same place two other ways besides that which came straight from the gate: one turned to the left hand, and the other to the right, at the bottom of the hill; but the narrow way lay right up the hill, and the name of the going up the side of the hill is called Difficulty. Christian now went to the spring, and drank thereof to refresh himself; and then he began to go up the hill, saying—

'The hill, though high, I covet to ascend;
The difficulty will not me offend;
For I perceive the way to life lies here.
Come, pluck up heart, let's neither faint nor fear;
Better, though difficult, the right way to go,
Than wrong, though easy, where the end is woe.'

The other two also came to the foot of the hill; but when they saw that the hill was steep and high, and that there were two other ways to go—and supposing also that these two ways might meet again with that up which Christian went, on the other side of the hill—therefore they were resolved to go in those ways. Now the name of one of those ways was Danger, and the name of the other Destruction. So the one took the way which is called Danger, which led him into a great wood; and the other took directly up the way to Destruction, which led him into a wide field, full of dark mountains, where he stumbled and fell, and rose no more.

I looked then after Christian, to see him go up the hill, where I perceived he fell from running to going, and from going to clambering upon his hands and his knees, because of the steepness of the place. Now, about the midway to the top of the hill was a pleasant arbour, made by the Lord of the hill for the refreshment of weary travellers. Thither, therefore, Christian got, where also he sat down to rest him. Then he pulled his roll out of his bosom, and read therein to his comfort.

The Pilgrim's Progress, John Bunyan, Collins, pages 56–57.

● ● ●

John Wesley wanted other people to have this feeling too. Whitefield had it. They had both become ministers of the Church of England and began preaching in the churches about the new birth, but the religious life of the Church had grown so cold that the members were blistered by the heat of this preaching and closed the pulpits to the Methodists. What then? "If the churches are closed, we will preach out of doors," said Whitefield and Wesley. They went to the people ... at the mouths of the coal pits as the miners went down or came up from work, to the villages of England. ...

The common people heard them gladly, and sometimes the audiences were as many as twenty and thirty thousand. But hoodlums tried to break up the meetings, by blowing horns, ringing bells, or hiring the town crier to bawl in front of the preacher. Sometimes cattle were driven into the congregation. Once a mob burst into the house where Wesley was staying. He walked into the thickest of them and called for a chair. "My heart was filled with love," he writes, "my eyes with tears, and my mouth with arguments.... They were amazed, they were ashamed, they melted down, they devoured every word. What a turn was this!" Wesley thanked God for getting together such a congregation of drunkards, swearers, and Sabbathbreakers.

Sometimes the bullies got caught in their own traps. Once a man in the crowd lifted his hand to throw a stone when another thrown from behind caught him right between the fingers. Another came with pockets full of rotten eggs. Wesley writes, "A young man coming unawares clapped his hands on each side, and mashed them all at once." And sometimes the bullies were themselves overcome by the man they were trying to crush. When a mob was nearly on the point of killing Wesley and a stout club had just missed his head, he began quietly to pray. Suddenly then the leader of the mob turned and said, "Sir, I will spend my life for you: follow me and not one soul here shall touch a hair of your head." They got out safely and that man became a leader in Methodism.

Wesley rode up and down England, Scotland, Wales, and Ireland, preaching in the fields and visiting the jails. He always traveled on horseback. In seven months he covered 2,400 miles and during his life 225,000 miles. Sometimes he made 90 miles in one day. He rode with a loose rein—that was the best way, he said, to keep a horse from stumbling, and as he rode he read history, poetry, philosophy, in English, in Latin, and in Greek.

By and by the tide turned and people began to admire him. Mayors offered him the freedom of the cities in which he had been mobbed. In his eighty-fifth year on visiting a certain town he wrote: "The last time I was here ... I was taken prisoner ... but how is the tide turned! High and low now lined the street, from one end of the town to the other, out of stark love and kindness...."

The Church of Our Fathers, Roland H. Bainton, Charles Scribner's Sons, pages 192–193.

● ● ●

All the way from Syria to Rome I have been chained to a detachment of soldiers who have behaved like animals towards me. I tried giving them money, but the more I gave them the more roughly they treated me. Quite honestly, they are like a pack of leopards, enjoying their role as hunters, with me as their prey.

Well, that has some advantages. I may as well get used to "leopards" now—it will be lions, and real ones at that, when I get to Rome. So I can make some progress towards preparing myself spiritually and mentally for what lies ahead.

All I pray is that when the moment comes the lions will be quick about it. Some Christians have suffered torments because the animals have toyed with them. If my lions are like that, I shall antagonize them!

Forgive me for writing like this, but I do know what is best for me. No power, human or spiritual, must hinder my coming to Jesus Christ. So whether the way be fire, or crucifixion, or wild beasts in the arena, or the mangling of my whole body, I can bear it, provided I am assured it is the way to him.

And it is! All the riches and power in the world cannot compare with that. So far as I am concerned, to die in Jesus Christ is better than to be king of the whole wide world! Do not try to tempt me to stay here by offering me the world and its attractions. Just let me make my way upward to that pure and undiluted light. For only when I get there will I truly be a *man.*

---

100 Days in the Arena, Ignatius of Antioch (c. A.D. 35–c. 107), David Winter, Harold Shaw, Day 37.

CHAPTER EIGHT

ENDORSING THE RIGHT LEADER

Who knew what was going to happen next? Events were unfolding at such a rapid pace. It was almost impossible to keep up with them, much less predict what the future would hold.

The sense that too much was occurring too fast had started with the untimely death of John the Baptist. After years of silence this prophetic voice had finally appeared on the scene. People flocked to hear him preach. Then just as suddenly as he came, he was gone. I'm confident the news of John's beheading was as shocking in that day as our being informed of the assassination of President Kennedy.

The prophetic void was quickly filled, however, by the even more popular teacher/miracle-worker from Nazareth. Large crowds followed Jesus everywhere, partly because of the healings He performed, but also because His words were electrifying. He talked openly, although somewhat guardedly, about His alternative kingship (or kingdom). The people seemed more than ready to support Him. Maybe they would have backed any messianic candidate who talked about release from Roman oppression.

Two men watched these unfolding events with great interest. If Jesus really was the Messiah, they had much to gain. If He wasn't, they had a great deal to lose.

Both were well off. One is called rich in Matthew's Gospel. He belonged among those who Jesus said would have a hard time making it into heaven. This man would beat the odds. But during these rapidly changing times, heaven must have seemed a long way off compared to more immediate concerns.

Each of these men was a member of the Sanhedrin, the Jewish council of supreme authority, though neither would be involved in the decision to put Christ to death. They struggled with whether to go out on a limb and support this man who appeared to be the promised Messiah, or to stall for time and pretend to ignore Him. Even today, sometimes it's hard to know if a new leader is worthy of our backing.

The reputation these two shared was that of being fine gentlemen. Luke writes that Joseph of Arimathea was good and righteous. John's Gospel presents Nicodemus as the finest of Pharisaism. He was a man you found it hard not to like.

Secret Disciples

Finally, we learn from John 19, that Joseph, like Nicodemus, was a secret disciple of Christ. Why secret? Because, like his friend, he feared his fellow Jews.

You can't really blame these men for being cautious. It would have been foolish to make a rash declaration of loyalty to Jesus. Probably the pressure to conform was greater than in any other culture. Among the Pharisees of Christ's day, the Jewish compliance knob had been turned from "hot" to "hottest." For either of these leaders to mention that he was considering endorsing the young preacher Jesus was to insure criticism from both friends and colleagues. It seems apparent they would feel pressure from a business perspective as well.

So Nicodemus and Joseph of Arimathea had quite understandably established a pattern of guarded carefulness. They wanted to be survivors. We see this policy emerging in John 3, where Nicodemus comes to Jesus at night. Of course in New Testament times evening hours were much darker than we now experience with the benefits of electricity, so Nicodemus could feel relatively sure his visit with Jesus would not be seen.

Later in John 7, the Pharisees ask the temple guards why they failed to carry out their orders and arrest Christ. They reply, "No one ever spoke the way this man does." The Pharisees respond angrily, "You mean He has deceived you also? . . . Has any of the rulers or of the Pharisees believed in Him?" (vv. 46-48)

Nicodemus, finding himself in that believing category, is reluctant to let such a statement go by without some kind of challenge. So he says, "Does our law condemn a man without first hearing him to find out what he is doing?" But the others react sarcastically, "Are you from Galilee, too? Look into it, and you will find that a prophet does not come out of Galilee" (vv. 51-52).

This rebuff was enough to keep Nicodemus from attempting any further verbal forays. After all, who enjoys being embarrassed or made to feel like the odd man out or considered non-kosher. Most people fear the opinions of others.

So Nicodemus left well enough alone. He tried to stop thinking so much about the young leader and His talk of an alternative kingdom. There was already enough fire under the pot. For the time being, Nicodemus' plan was to keep playing by the Roman rules and to guard his ties to the status quo. He would do what he could to see that Jesus' followers remained passive, that the crowds did not get out of hand and start an uprising.

But suddenly the time arrived for this cautious twosome, Joseph of Arimathea and Nicodemus, to consider a change. You see, the level of their own *internal* unrest had also been building. It reached a peak the horrible afternoon when Christ was crucified. Maybe our two conscientious subjects felt particularly responsible for Jesus' death because they had passively allowed it to happen.

Here then were two quality individuals, bound by a fear of those whose opinions differed from theirs in reference to the Messiah. But these two were about to discover that an opportunity had come up that required a special service from them both. God was calling them to be His men in His place in His time.

Everything was happening so quickly there was barely time to think. Christ had been arrested Thursday evening in the garden. The trial followed immediately in the early hours of the next day, and our Lord was nailed to the cross by noon on Friday. Within a short time He was dead.

Now what was to be done with the mangled body of the Son of God? His twelve disciples were Galileans, except for

Judas. None of them owned a burial place in Jerusalem. And there was hardly time before sundown, which began the Sabbath, to purchase a tomb. Besides, most of the disciples were in hiding.

Special Assignments

Almost as soon as our two secret believers began to talk about what had happened, they were aware that an extended discussion would be fruitless. That's because a voice within had already said, "Joseph, I'm ready to use that new tomb you purchased—for My Son. And Nicodemus, I'm going to need the help of your burial skills. Now, I assume you men will accept these special assignments."

I can almost hear Joseph's reaction: "All right, all right, God. Just give us a little time to figure out how we can pull this off secretly. Because if our peers find out, they're sure to be offended. Let's see now, my new tomb. Um, that's a tough one."

Then I imagine Nicodemus quickly adding, "I fear our 'nice guy' days have come to an end, Joseph. Didn't I hear you talking to several in the Sanhedrin about buying that tomb? I sense that from this day on, everything will be out in the open. And I see dire consequences resulting from our actions."

"Yes, my friend," might respond Joseph, "but I feel a worse judgment will be upon us if we fail to do what God wants."

Mark 15:43 is a great verse. In fact, it's one of my favorites. It reads, "Joseph of Arimathea, a prominent member of the Council [and that's half of the classic conflict, the fear of man], who was himself waiting for the kingdom of God [there's the other half, the offense of the Gospel], went *boldly* to Pilate and asked for Jesus' body" (italics added). So Joseph mustered his courage and took a stand.

Maybe Joseph's mastering of the moment was all the encouragement Nicodemus needed because in John 19:39-40 we see that "He [Joseph] was accompanied by Nicodemus, the man who earlier had visited Jesus at night. Nicodemus brought a mixture of myrrh and aloes, about seventy-five pounds."

Dear men, weren't they? I feel like applauding them! It took real courage to come out into the open and declare their loyalties.

They didn't know what the future would bring. They probably had no thoughts whatever of a resurrection. But they went on record as being men who were openly on Jesus' side. They said in essence, "When our names come up, Joseph of Arimathea and Nicodemus, people will say we are unashamedly Christian."

I make a point of this because these men differed from their colleagues. When almost everyone else in the Sanhedrin remained opposed to Christ, these two made the right choice. In spite of the confusion of the day, they were able to see clearly that Jesus was exactly who He claimed to be, the Son of Almighty God. And they believed and followed Him regardless of the cost.

Endorse the Right Leader

Because the future is unpredictable, it's especially important to endorse the right leader. That's a survival skill. Follow the wrong person and who knows where he or she will lead you, especially in a time like the present.

Recently I was searching for a good word to describe our times. What I came up with was *portentous*. A portent is like having a massive dark cloud appearing before a storm. In portentous times we feel uneasy because we don't know whether we're ready for what's coming. A portentous day is the opposite of a sunshiny, let's-go-on-a-picnic kind of day.

That's how I see our world. Its changes and churnings are coming closer daily to where we live. Events are happening so fast it's hard to adjust to them all. It's too much, too fast. That's why the topic of survival skills is so timely.

Too many issues beyond our sphere of influence impact our lives. For example, we don't personally control the ozone layer or the earth's deforestation rate or the proliferation of nations possessing nuclear weapons. These and numerous other concerns are someone else's responsibility. Most of us are not world leaders.

A leader is someone others will follow to a place they

wouldn't go on their own. If for some reason people refuse to follow a given individual, he or she is no longer a leader. In a portentous day it's important to decide whether the leaders we're following are worthy of our trust.

Sometimes I feel a little like the puppet Pinocchio. I'm a newcomer in a fast-moving world which I don't understand all that well, and I'm prone to make a lot of mistakes.

Remember the story of Carlo Lorenzini, who used the pen name Collodi? In his mid-fifties he began a serial called *The Tale of a Puppet* for a childrens' weekly. Two years later the series was published as a book, and like so many classics it proved delightful for children of all ages.

A friend of mine who is a Church of God minister, Dr. David New, shared with me how he illustrated a sermon with scenes from the Disney film *Pinocchio*. That brought to mind cartoon memories of old Geppetto the woodcarver, Figaro his cat, Cleo the goldfish, and Jiminy Cricket singing "When You Wish upon a Star."

In the story, it is the loving wish of the old man "that Pinocchio would become a real live boy." And that's what happens.

"I can talk," the puppet exclaims with joy. "I can walk." The only thing he is missing is a conscience, and that's the role the cricket is to play on his behalf.

The very next morning, Pinocchio is sent on his way to school, books under his arm. Is the little fellow ready for what's to come?

Oh, no! He's just been tripped by a fox, J. Worthington Foulfellow, and his raunchy little sidekick, Gideon the cat. They tell Pinocchio that school is not where he should be. It's a waste of his time. Instead he needs to meet Stromboli, the circus master. A puppet with no strings would be the star of the circus.

"What's all this nonsense about the stage?" shouts an angry Jiminy Cricket. "Think of your Papa, Geppetto!" But Pinocchio is stagestruck. What is it he sings as he dances in the circus? "Ain't no strings on me!" He takes his bows amid a shower of gold coins—which Stromboli keeps. Then Stromboli mistreats his star puppet, threatening to use him as firewood. Between performances he keeps him locked in a cage.

Later that night, Jiminy Cricket slips into the room and climbs up to the cage. "So this is how you become a star," he whispers, shaking his head.

Following the wrong person is a mistake easily made by someone like Pinocchio, who's new in the process of becoming a real person. Hopefully, though, we all learn our lesson after a couple of painful blunders.

In our society a lot of individuals have been tripped up lately, not only by the desire for money or the applause of their peers, but also by supposed religious leaders. I guess that was inevitable. Sooner or later in a secular culture, where the supernatural is viewed more or less as irrelevant, people begin to long for something beyond themselves, outside the realm of mere humanity. And of course not everything that's passed off today as spiritual is worth following.

On the positive side, Jesus is a personality to whom many are flocking. Outside North America He is drawing a huge following. In fact, this openness to the Lord is unprecedented in the history of the world.

Many of us have been hoping that in North America there will also be a new sense of receptivity toward Christ. We pray continually for revival in the churches throughout the states and provinces.

Revival always begins among Christians. It's marked by a new commitment to Jesus and His teachings. Christians know they should follow Christ closely, yet sometimes it seems so hard to do what we know would be to our benefit.

On a true-false quiz, believers would easily answer the following questions correctly.

True or false: It is in your best interest to pick and choose which teachings of Christ you want to obey.

You know that's false.

Here's another.

True or false: It is wise to live in accordance with all that Jesus taught.

That's another easy one. It's obviously true.

We can answer the questions, but it's another thing to pull our lives in line with those directives and not just say, "I'm a

Christian," but actually follow hard after Christ.

Like Joseph of Arimathea and Nicodemus, we're pretty well convinced that Jesus is who He claimed to be, the unique Son of God, but we have a hard time letting that truth impact our lives the way it should.

That's why we struggle with disciplines like downscaling.

That's why we let stress get to us rather than off-loading it onto Christ.

That's why we copy our society and remain individualistic, resisting helpful ideas like combining resources.

That's why we fight for our own rights, barely listening to the other person's position, much less the pain behind it.

That's why our sense of dignity is often more related to what people think about us than to what God thinks.

That's why we sometimes forget we're not infinite as God is, so we don't set proper limits on what we can do.

That's why we don't like to identify with the suffering of Christ.

Oh, we make excuses for our actions. We're like Pinocchio when the Blue Fairy asked why he was locked in the cage. "Oh, it wasn't my fault," he replied, "A giant monster with bulging eyes kidnapped me!"

"And what about school?"

"School? Ah, well, that was lots of fun."

With each lie, Pinocchio's nose grew longer, until it stretched right through the bars of the cage.

"Now you see, Pinocchio," the Blue Fairy explained, "a lie grows and grows until it's as plain as the nose on your face."

Most Christians haven't yet come to this understanding. We still live under the illusion that all is relatively well, that the church really isn't backslidden! Though our nose is seen as disproportionately long by outsiders, within the church we've gotten rather used to its length.

"A few changes here or there," we think, "and we'll be all right. The problem will just take a couple of minor adjustments."

I believe otherwise. Even the simple alterations suggested in this book will seem radical to many.

Here's the bottom line. First we need to decide whether

the dark clouds are real. Is the forecast for tomorrow good or bad? Maybe it's still picnic time! Or are we living in a portentous day?

If the times are ominous, whose leadership will we endorse? Whose petition will we sign our name to? Who will get our approval and commitment? When none of our human leaders seem to be adequate for the tasks at hand, do we say that's how we feel about Jesus too?

My conviction is that this is a time to live decidedly Christian, to be unashamedly Christian, to feel enthusiastically Christian. We must forget about whether others think we're nice people and instead be concerned only that they know we place our total confidence in Christ—in who He is and in everything He says. Let's listen to the voice in our conscience, the Holy Spirit, that says, "I'm ready now to use the resources entrusted to you. This is the time you're to respond."

"Yes," we reply. "We're ready to follow You, Jesus, even to places we wouldn't normally go on our own."

FOR DISCUSSION AND REFLECTION

1.   When was a time you were burned because you followed a leader unworthy of your trust?

2.   What are the major qualities you look for in a leader?

3.   If you sometimes hesitate to follow Christ's words, do you know why this is?

4.   What major qualities do you think the Son of God looks for in His followers?

5.   How important is it to you that the earthly leaders you endorse are Christian?

6.   Name several situations where failing to endorse the right leader could threaten survival.

READINGS

The authorities banned Jesus from teaching in the synagogue for his flagrant breach of Sabbath regulations. They did not excommunicate him nor sentence him to be whipped, but they marked him publicly as in disgrace. Privately, they began to think of ways to murder him. Those who kept him company would lose their good names and perhaps their lives.

A few evenings later Jesus instructed Peter and John to pass the word that early next morning he would teach at a lonely spot above Capernaum. He went away by himself, ordering them on no account to follow him into the hills, while they visited or sent messages to all in the neighborhood who regularly sat at his feet. At first light they found that some had excused themselves, but seventy or eighty of the more eager were walking up the mountain, unaware why Jesus wanted them.

When they breasted the rise to the chosen little plateau, John saw Jesus on a rock looking out across the lake below, which sparkled in the summer morning sun before the heat haze blurred the view. He seemed bathed in sunshine, but as they came closer, John realized that Jesus' face and eyes shone with an inner light; he must have spent the night in prayer.

Once they had gathered round him, Jesus explained his purpose. He was about to choose twelve men to work at his side, or occasionally to go elsewhere on his behalf and learn more than he could impart to crowds.

John's heart missed a beat or two as he waited to hear whether he would be one of the Twelve. First Jesus called out Simon Peter's name, and immediately, with a characteristic touch, put Andrew's fear at rest by telling him to join his brother. When John heard his own older brother named, his doubts dissolved, and a few moments later he was with James at Jesus' side. Jesus next called the friends of the walk to Cana from Jordan's bank, Philip and Bartholomew-Nathanael;

then Matthew, and five more. Only one of the Twelve was not a Galilean. His name was Judas Iscariot, "the man from Kerioth," a town on the plateau to the east of the Dead Sea. Nothing about Judas gave a hint to the eleven others that the seeds of treachery were in him.

John was almost overcome by excitement, by feelings of privilege and gratitude, and a determination to be worthy. On the other hand, Jesus conveyed the unspoken sense that the privilege of having the Twelve was his, that each was a gift entrusted to him for their sakes as much as for his.

The Master, John Pollock, Victor Books, 1983, pages 47–48.

● ● ●

My introspection plumbed the secret depths and brought together all my misery in plain sight of my heart, so that a great storm broke, bringing a shower of tears. In order to pour out the whole tempest without holding back, I got up and walked away from Alypius, as it seemed to me that solitude was the best climate for the business of crying. I went to a corner of the garden where I wouldn't be bothered by his presence. He sensed what my feelings were, for I probably said something in which the choking in my voice told that I was on the verge of tears. So I left, and he sat there more dumbfounded than ever.

In some way, I'm not just sure how, I threw myself down under a fig tree and let the tears gush freely. These were the streams that proved a sacrifice acceptable to you, my Lord. Not in the exact words of Scripture but in some similar vein I talked with you for a long time. I asked, "And thou, Lord, how long wilt thou be roused to such fury? Do not remember the sins of former times"—for I felt they were still holding me. I ended on a dismal note: "How long, how long? Tomorrow and tomorrow? Why not now? Why not put an end to my sin right this hour?"

I was going on like this, weeping in bitter dejection of spirit, when I heard a voice coming from the house next door. Whether it was a boy's or a girl's I don't know, but it was singing over and over in a kind of chant, "Take up and read, take up and read." Immediately my demeanor changed. I thought back over the children's games I knew, trying to recall whether I had ever heard such an expression used. I knew of no such game. Stanching the flow of tears, I stood up, for I could only interpret the words as a kind of divine command to open the Scripture and read the first passage I came across. I had heard how Anthony once dropped in unexpectedly at a church service during a reading of the gospel, and was inspired by what he heard as if it were addressed to him personally: "Go and sell what you have and give it to the poor, and you shall have treasure in heaven; and come and follow me." By this word from the Lord he was converted to you right on the spot. So I returned quickly to the bench where Alypius was sitting. When I had moved from there I'd left behind the copy of the letters of the Apostle. Now I grabbed up the book, opened it, and read silently the first portion of Scripture on which my eyes lighted: "Not in reveling and drunkenness, not in debauchery and licentiousness, not in quarreling and jealousy. But put on the Lord Jesus Christ, and make no provision for the flesh to gratify its desires." I had no need or wish to read further, for when I came to the end of the sentence, instantly, it seemed, a light of certainty turned on in my heart and all the fog of doubt disappeared.

Then marking the place by inserting my finger between the pages or in some way or other, I shut the book and in a tranquil frame of mind told Alypius what had happened. He confided something of what had been occupying his own thoughts—which I knew nothing about. He asked to see what I had just been reading and I showed him. He then looked beyond the passage. I had no idea what followed, but it was this: "As for the man who is weak in faith, welcome him." Alypius told me he applied those words to himself. They provided motive power to strengthen his determination to resolve his own situation and—without stalling and without making waves—to join me in a good purpose. It was just like him to do it, for his moral character had been better than mine for a long, long time.

We went into the house and gave my mother the news and she was overjoyed. When we explained to her how it had all come about, she was exuberant and triumphant and gave thanks to you who are "able to do far more abundantly than all that we ask or think." She saw that you had given her, on my behalf, far more than she was used to asking for in all her sobbings and groanings and wailings. You had converted me to yourself on the same rule of faith you had revealed to her for so many years before, and had turned all her mourning into gladness.

_____

Love Song, Augustine's Confession for Modern Man, Sherwood Eliot Wirt, Harper & Row, pages 116–118.

● ● ●

He closed the door of the lecture-room and went and stood before the little group. His face was pale and his lips trembled with genuine emotion. It was to him a genuine crisis in his own life and that of his parish. No man can tell until he is moved by the Divine Spirit what he may do, or how he may change the current of a lifetime of fixed habits of thought and speech and action. Henry Maxwell did not, as we have said, yet know himself all that he was passing through, but he was conscious of a great upheaval in his definition of Christian discipleship, and he was moved with a depth of feeling he could not measure as he looked into the faces of those men and women on this occasion.

It seemed to him that the most fitting word to be spoken first was that of prayer. He asked them all to pray with him. And almost with the first syllable he uttered there was a distinct presence of the Spirit felt by them all. As the prayer went on, the presence grew in power. They all felt it. The room was filled with it as plainly as if it had been visible. When the prayer closed there was a silence that lasted several moments. All the heads were bowed. Henry Maxwell's face was wet with tears. If an audible voice from heaven had sanctioned their pledge to follow the Master's steps, not one person present could have felt more certain of the divine blessing. And so the most serious movement ever started in the First Church of Raymond was begun.

"We all understand," said he, speaking very quietly, "what we have undertaken to do. We pledge ourselves to do everything in our daily lives after asking the question, 'What would Jesus do?' regardless of what may be the result to us. Some time I shall be able to tell you what a marvelous change has come over my life within a week's time. I cannot now. But the experience I have been through since last Sunday has left me so dissatisfied with my previous definition of Christian discipleship that I have been compelled to take this action. I did not dare begin it alone. I know that I am being led by the hand of divine love in all this. The same divine impulse must have led you also.

"Do we understand fully what we have undertaken?"

"I want to ask a question," said Rachel Winslow. Every one turned towards her. . . .

"I am a little in doubt as to the source of our knowledge concerning what Jesus would do. Who is to decide for me just what He would do in my case? It is a different age. There are many perplexing questions in our civilization that are not mentioned in the teachings of Jesus. How am I going to tell what He would do?"

"There is no way that I know of," replied the pastor, "except as we study Jesus through the medium of the Holy Spirit. You remember what Christ said speaking to His disciples about the Holy Spirit: 'Howbeit when He the spirit of truth is come, He shall guide you into all the truth; for He shall not speak for Himself; but what things soever He shall hear, there shall He speak; and He shall declare unto you the things that are to come. He shall glorify me; for He shall take of mine and declare it unto you. All things whatsoever the Father hath are mine; therefore said I, that He taketh of mine and shall declare it unto you.' There is no other test that I know of. We shall all have to decide what Jesus would do after going to that source of knowledge."

"What if others say of us, when we do certain things, that Jesus would not do so?" asked the superintendent of railroads.

"We cannot prevent that. But we must be absolutely honest with ourselves. The standard of Christian action cannot vary in most of our acts."

"And yet what one church member thinks Jesus would do, another refuses to accept as His probable course of action. What is to render our conduct uniformly Christ-like? Will it be possible to reach the same conclusion always in all cases?" asked President Marsh.

Mr. Maxwell was silent some time. Then he answered, "No; I don't know that we can expect that. But when it comes to a genuine, honest, enlightened following of Jesus' steps, I cannot believe there will be any confusion either in our own minds or in the judgment of others. We must be free from fanaticism on one hand and too much caution on the other. If Jesus' example is the example for the world to follow, it certainly must be feasible to follow it. But we need to remember this great fact. After we have asked the Spirit to tell us what Jesus would do and have received an answer to it, we are to act regardless of the results to ourselves. Is that understood?"

In His Steps, Charles Sheldon, Word, pages 16–18.

At the conclusion of the service, Dr. Walter Wilson and his father-in-law, who had attended the meeting with him, returned home. Each went at once to his own room. Utterly heartbroken over his fruitless life, yet filled with a great hope because of the message he had heard from a teacher in whom he had all confidence, Dr. Wilson lay upon the carpet of his study, prostrate in God's presence. Hear his testimony:

There, in the quiet of that late hour, I said to the Holy Spirit, "My Lord, I have mistreated You all my Christian life. I have treated You like a servant. When I wanted You I called for You; when I was about to engage in some work I beckoned You to come and help me perform my task. I have kept You in the place of a servant.

I have sought to use You only as a willing servant to help me in my self-appointed and chosen work. I shall do so no more. Just now I give You this body of mine; from my head to my feet, I give it to You. I give You my hands, my limbs, my eyes and lips, my brain; all that I am within and without, I hand over to You for You to live in it the life that You please. You may send this body to Africa, or lay it on a bed with cancer. You may blind the eyes, or send me with Your message to Tibet. You may take this body to the Eskimos, or send it to a hospital with pneumonia. It is Your body from this moment on. Help Yourself to it. Thank You, my Lord, I believe You have accepted it, for in Romans twelve and one You said, "acceptable unto God." Thank You again, my Lord, for taking me. We now belong to each other."

And what were the results of that surrender of body and appropriation of the fullness of the Holy Spirit?

The very next morning two young ladies came to the office to sell advertising, as they had done previously. Up to that time the doctor had never spoken to them about the Lord Jesus because his lips had been his own and he had used them for business purposes. Now that his lips had been given away, the Holy Spirit was to use them; and He did so at once. Out of brief conversation and testimony to his visitors, Dr. Wilson led both of them to a saving knowledge of Jesus Christ. They were the first fruits of a great harvest of souls that Dr. Wilson has won for the Saviour.

They Found the Secret, V. Raymond Edman, Zondervan, pages 126–127.

● ● ●

From that moment life was unified in one great purpose and prayer. For Hudson Taylor was "not disobedient to the heavenly vision," and to him obedience to the will of God was a very practical matter. At once he began to prepare, as well as he could, for a life that would call for physical endurance. He took more exercise in the open air, exchanged his feather bed for a hard mattress and was watchful not to be self-indulgent at table. Instead of going to church twice on Sunday, he gave up the evening to visiting in the poorest parts of the town, distributing tracts and holding cottage-meetings. In crowded lodging-house kitchens he became a welcome figure, and even on the race course his bright face and kindly words opened the way for many a straight message. All this led to more Bible study and prayer, for he soon found that there is One and One alone who can make us "fishers of men."

The study of Chinese, also, was entered upon with ardour. A grammar of that formidable language would have cost more than twenty dollars and a dictionary at least seventy-five. He could afford neither. But with a copy of the Gospel of Luke in Chinese, by patiently comparing brief verses with their equivalent in English, he found out the meaning of more than six hundred characters. These he learned and made into a dictionary of his own, carrying on at the same time other lines of study.

I have begun to get up at five in the morning [he wrote to his sister at school] and find it necessary to go to bed early. I must study if I mean to go to China. I am fully decided to go, and am making every preparation I can. I intend to rub up my Latin, to learn Greek and the rudiments of Hebrew, and get as much general information as possible. I need your prayers.

Several years with his father as a dispensing chemist had increased his desire to study medicine, and when an opportunity occurred of becoming assistant to a leading physician in Hull he was not slow to avail himself of it. This meant leaving the home circle, but first in the doctor's residence and later in the home of an aunt, his mother's sister, the young assistant was still surrounded with refinement and comfort.

This proved, indeed, one of the elements in the new life which led him to serious thinking. Dr. Hardey paid a salary sufficient to cover personal expenses, but Hudson Taylor was giving, as a matter of duty and privilege, a tenth of all that came to him to the work of God. He was devoting time on Sunday to evangelism in a part of the town where there was urgent need for temporal as well as spiritual help. And this raised the question, why should he not spend less for himself and have the joy of giving more to others?

On the outskirts of the town, beyond some vacant lots, a double row of cottages bordered a narrow canal which gave the name of "Drainside" to the none-too-attractive neighborhood. The canal was just a deep ditch into which Drainside people were in the habit of throwing rubbish to be carried away, in part, whenever the tide rose high enough—for Hull is a seaport town. The cottages, like peas in a pod, followed the windings of the Drain for half a mile or so, each having one door and two windows. It was for a rented room in one of these little places that Hudson Taylor left his aunt's pleasant home on Charlotte Street. Mrs. Finch, his landlady, was a true Christian and delighted to have "the young doctor" under her roof. She did her best, no doubt, to make the chamber clean and comfortable, polishing the fireplace opposite the window and making up the bed in the corner farthest from the door. A plain deal table and a chair or two completed the appointments. The room was only twelve feet square and did not need much furniture. It was on a level with the ground and opened familiarly out of the kitchen. From the window one looked across to "The Founder's Arms," a countrified public-house whose lights were useful on dark nights shining across the mud and water of the Drain.

Whatever it may have been in summer, toward the close of November when Hudson Taylor made it his home Drainside must have seemed dreary enough. To add to the changed conditions he was boarding himself, which meant that he bought his meager supplies as he returned from the surgery and rarely sat down to a proper meal. His walks were solitary, his evenings spent alone, and Sundays brought long hours of work in his district or among the crowds who frequented the Humber Dock.

Having now the twofold object in view [he recalled] of accustoming myself to endure hardness, and of economizing in order to help those among whom I was labouring in the Gospel, I soon found that I could live upon very much less than I had previously thought possible. Butter, milk, and other luxuries I ceased to use, and found that by living mainly on oatmeal and rice, with occasional variations, a very small sum was sufficient for my needs. In this way I had more than two-thirds of my income available for other purposes, and my experience was that the less I spent on myself and the more I gave to others, the fuller of happiness and blessing did my soul become.

For God is no man's debtor, and here in his solitude Hudson Taylor was learning something of what He can be to the one who follows hard after Him.

Hudson Taylor's Spiritual Secret, Dr. and Mrs. Howard Taylor, China Inland Mission, pages 17–19.